Harmony in the Hive

HARMONY
IN
THE HIVE

A Vibrant Vision
for Freemasonry's Future

Nathan A. St. Pierre

with a foreword by

Jacob M. Bressman

Plumbstone
WASHINGTON, D.C.

Cover emblem by Thomas J. Grylls.

Frontispiece illustration copyright © 2024 by Nathalie Strassburg.

Publisher's Cataloging-in-Publication data

St. Pierre, Nathan A., 1984–
    Harmony in the Hive: A Vibrant Vision for Freemasonry's Future /
    by Nathan A. St. Pierre; foreword by Jacob M. Bressman. — 1st ed.
    181 p.   23 cm.   Includes bibliographical references.
    ISBN-13 978-1-60302-089-3 (hardcover)
    ISBN-13 978-1-60302-088-6 (pbk.)
    ISBN-13 978-1-60302-090-9 (ebook)
    ISBN-13 978-1-60302-091-6 (audiobook)

    1. Freemasonry—United States. 2. Freemasonry—History.
    3. Freemasons—Conduct of life. 4. Freemasonry—Philosophy.
    5. Masonic symbolism.
    I. Title.

HS395 .S74 2024   366.1

http://plumbstone.com

This book is dedicated
to the author of the book not yet written.

W. Kirk MacNulty inspired me.
W. Arthur Ralph inspired him.
They were both inspired by W. L. Wilmshurst.

May this work in some way inspire you
to contribute to the common stock.

Contents

PART IV
Restoring Harmony in the Lodge

Foreword

FREEMASONRY, AT ITS CORE, is a living tradition of spiritual reflection, philosophical inquiry, and moral discipline. This work, *Harmony in the Hive*, masterfully revives the ancient lessons embedded in one of Masonry's most evocative symbols— the beehive. This image, rich with historical resonance, is not merely an emblem of industrious labor but an esoteric guide for understanding the delicate interplay between unity and individuality, practicality and spirituality, structure and harmony.

The beehive, like a Masonic lodge, demands balance. Each bee contributes its share toward the collective good, yet the sweetness it produces—honey—reminds us that labor should never be mechanical or devoid of meaning. True labor involves more than action; it requires an intentional pursuit of wisdom, personal growth, and fraternity. This text urges us to return to these deeper meanings within Freemasonry, inviting us to examine our own practices and rituals.

Through the lens of the beehive, *Harmony in the Hive* guides us to recognize that the Craft's survival does not lie in superficial reforms, nor in merely recruiting members to fill vacant chairs. Instead, this work presents a blueprint for restoring vibrancy within the fraternity by rediscovering the deeper purposes that have sustained Freemasonry for centuries: intellectual engagement, moral instruction, and spiritual reflection.

Freemasonry is both operative and speculative, both body and soul. In the beehive metaphor, this duality becomes clear. The practical work of building and maintaining lodges, mirrors the bees' hive-building, but this practical labor must align with the speculative, inner work of self-improvement. In Masonry, the tools of the architect—the square, the compasses, and the plumb—are also symbols of spiritual refinement. The same is true for the beehive: it exemplifies not only labor but also unity, order, and the moral lessons drawn from these concepts.

Historically, the beehive has served as a symbol of sacred order across civilizations—from ancient Egypt's use of the bee as a royal emblem to the spiritual significance attributed to bees in Classical and British folklore. Bees were thought to carry messages from the divine, embody souls, or symbolize immortality. Likewise, Freemasonry seeks to guide its members towards enlightenment and moral immortality through the teachings conveyed in rituals. As this text shows, the connection between the hive and the Lodge reveals much about how Masonry's ancient wisdom aligns with the rhythms of the natural world and the spiritual cosmos.

Yet, as *Harmony in the Hive* reminds us, the beehive also warns against complacency. Just as worker bees expel drones from the hive when they cease to contribute, Freemasonry must remain vigilant in cultivating engagement and warding off stagnation. Intellectual laziness, ritual carelessness, and passive membership undermines the Craft's integrity. Each Mason, like each bee, must play an active role, not merely for personal gain but to ensure that the lodge thrives as a center of learning, brotherhood, and virtue.

The challenges facing modern Freemasonry—declining membership, disengaged brethren, and a fractured connection between tradition and innovation—cannot be solved by simple administrative measures. Instead, we must reclaim our esoteric heritage and foster a culture that prizes both personal development and collective harmony. The beehive offers a compelling model for this renewal. It reminds us that industriousness is not measured in busyness, but rather in the quality of what we produce—whether in intellectual endeavors, moral improvement, or ritual performance.

Freemasonry's speculative tradition teaches that enlightenment is a process, not a destination. *Harmony in the Hive* beautifully illustrates this truth by showing how each generation of Masons must continue the labor of previous generations while adapting the Craft's teachings to new circumstances. As we approach a new era in Masonry, we are challenged to revisit our rituals, practices, and educational programs with fresh eyes, rebalancing the operative and speculative aspects of our work. This book emphasizes that the lessons of the beehive extend beyond the walls of the lodge. A vibrant Masonic culture requires alignment between the inner and outer worlds—between contemplation and action, between self-improvement and service to the world around us. By applying the beehive's principles, Freemasonry can once again become a beacon of wisdom, unity, and moral leadership in a fragmented world.

Ultimately, *Harmony in the Hive* calls each of us to consider our role in preserving and advancing the Craft. The beehive teaches that the success of the whole depends on the contributions of each member. In this spirit, let us recommit ourselves to the ideals of Freemasonry: laboring not for personal gain, but for the greater good of humanity; seeking knowledge not for its own sake, but for the light it brings to the soul; and building a community that reflects the harmony we hope to see in the world.

Harmony in the Hive offers us not only a reflection on where Freemasonry stands today but also a guide for how it can flourish tomorrow. It is a reminder that the tools we need are already in our hands and that the design for the future is already laid upon the Trestleboard. Let us now begin the work.

Jacob Bressman
Grand Master, 2024
The Grand Lodge, F.A.A.M.,
of the District of Columbia

Publisher's Foreword

IN THE RICH SYMBOLISM of the Masonic tradition, the beehive is employed as a reminder to all that it is essential that the initiate endeavors to contribute to the "common stock of knowledge," and one who refuses to do so is described in the same homily as a mere "drone in the hive of nature, a useless member of society, and unworthy of our protection as Masons." It is one of the most pointed warnings uttered during the initiate's tutelage, and it is admittedly puzzling that many participants in the institution express unfamiliarity with this explicit demand to engage in a communal pursuit of wisdom.

This disconnection between foundational principles and contemporary practice exemplifies a broader pattern of drift from the institution's original purposes. It is unlikely that attempts to address Freemasonry's perceived deficits will be effective unless they are grounded in the essentials of Masonic tradition. Superficial adjustments to form without attention to these fundamental precepts will inevitably fall short. Only a revitalization based upon substance is worthy of serious consideration, and in these pages Nathan St. Pierre presents ideas that will prove profoundly effective among any who put them into practice. *Sic vos non vobis mellificatis apes.*

Shawn Eyer
The Harvard Lodge
Boston, Massachusetts

Acknowledgments

THIS WORK, LIKE THE BEEHIVE it examines, is the product of many industrious laborers. While I have gathered and arranged the materials herein, the honey of wisdom it contains has been collected from countless flowers in the garden of Masonic knowledge.

First and foremost, I must acknowledge the Great Architect of the Universe, without whose divine guidance this labor could not have been accomplished. Like the bee that instinctively knows its way home to the hive, I have been blessed with direction when the path seemed unclear.

My sincere gratitude extends to the brethren of Federal Lodge № 1 who answered when I knocked. Thank you for making me a Mason and providing a practical foundation for this work.

All of my heart belongs to my beloved Lodge of the Nine Muses № 1776 who had for so long been a single glimmering ray in the darkness. Thank you for trusting me with the gavel for four and a half of the most spiritually fulfilling years of my life.

My profound thanks also go to the brethren of Melbourne Lodge № 143 who remind me on a weekly basis that it doesn't matter how many books I write; I still have to learn to subdue my passions and improve myself in Masonry.

Special thanks must go to Shawn Eyer, FPS, whose deep understanding of Masonic Tradition first sparked my interest in writing. His stewardship of *Philalethes: The Journal of Masonic Research and*

Letters and willingness to share his knowledge exemplify the true spirit of Masonic education.

I am deeply indebted to the scholars whose work has illuminated the path before me. The writings of William Preston, Walter Leslie Wilmshurst, and W. Kirk MacNulty have been invaluable guides in understanding the philosophical dimensions of our Craft. The contemporary research of Shawn Eyer and Christopher B. Murphy has provided crucial insights into early Grand Lodge era Freemasonry that have shaped this work.

To Luke Young, 33°, and Grant Haver on whose thoughtful feedback I have relied for years. Our discussions about the future of the Craft have helped shape many of the ideas presented here.

My deepest appreciation goes to my family, who have patiently supported my countless hours of research and writing. Like the quiet strength of the hive supporting its workers, your love and understanding have made this work possible.

Finally, to all the brethren who labor daily to preserve and transmit the Light of Freemasonry to future generations—this work is dedicated to you. May it serve as one small contribution to the great work of keeping our beloved Craft vital and meaningful in the modern world.

Any errors or oversights in this work are entirely my own. Like the bee that sometimes strays from its intended flower, I may have wandered from perfect accuracy. I welcome fraternal correction and dialogue as we all strive to build our symbolic temple.

Nathan St. Pierre, Ph.D.
November 2024
Florida

The Hive Prepares for Winter

An Introduction

THE GREATEST GIFT a fraternity can give is its members. I recall one beloved Mason; he spoke of a schoolteacher, someone from a neighboring state, who had long cherished the hope of becoming a Master Mason. After much anticipation, his petition was finally accepted, and he presented himself for the Entered Apprentice degree. The night of his initiation, however, turned out to be his last encounter with the Lodge. He never returned.

At first, the brethren thought they had simply misjudged the man's interest in Freemasonry. But, as my companion explained, this wasn't the case. The problem wasn't a lack of interest—it was disillusionment. The Master of the Lodge had conducted the degree with such carelessness and lack of preparation that it was more of an insult than an initiation. A good man was lost to Freemasonry, not because he lacked the heart for it, but because the Lodge leadership lacked respect for the ritual.

This story, for many of you, will feel almost too familiar, too relevant to what we still see today in Lodges across the country. For others of you, it will feel more familiar still, for this was not just a casual tale—it belongs to Dwight L. Smith, Past Grand Master of

Indiana, who published it in 1963.[1] In this work—titled *Whither Are We Travelling*—Smith warned of the same complacency, carelessness, and loss of true meaning that threatens the Craft today.

It's a reminder that the problems Freemasonry faces in the twenty-first century are not new. The disillusionment caused by unprepared leadership and neglected rituals is part of a broader issue—one that spans decades and, in fact, can be traced back to the mid-twentieth century. The period following World War II, often considered the "Golden Age" of Freemasonry, was soon followed by what can only be described as an Era of Decline. Membership numbers across the United States have steadily dwindled since the 1950s, bringing Freemasonry to the present situation.

While many bemoan the dropping numbers, Smith's cautionary tale reminds us that this crisis isn't simply about recruiting new members; it's about cultivating an experience that is worthy of the Craft. The numbers tell one story, but the real issue lies deeper, in how we honor—and sometimes neglect—the traditions that make Freemasonry what it is.

The State of the Bees

Freemasons initiated at the dawn of the twenty-first century have been repeatedly confronted with apocalyptic declarations regarding the fraternity's dwindling numbers. For many within the Craft, these warnings initially appeared overstated, even melodramatic. However, as the first quarter of the century draws to a close, the once-dismissed concerns have proven more grounded in reality. The steady decline in Freemasonry's membership across the United States, which began in the mid-twentieth century, now seems an ir-

1   Dwight L. Smith, "Whither Are We Travelling," *Ars Quatuor Coronatorum, Being the Transactions of the Quatuor Coronati Lodge No. 2076* 76 (1963): 36.

reversible trend. While the largest Grand Lodges—with over 100,000 members—have perhaps been the loudest in their alarm, the medium, small, and even the smallest Grand Lodges are no less affected.

According to data from the Masonic Service Association of North America (MSANA), Freemasonry in the U.S. peaked in 1959 with over 4.1 million members.[2] By 1963, the renowned Indiana Mason Dwight L. Smith had already voiced concerns about the decline. A forward thinker, Smith's critiques of complacency within the fraternity resonate more today than perhaps they did in his time. When Smith laid down his working tools in 1993, the fraternity had 2.3 million members in the United States. By 2013, membership had fallen to approximately 1.2 million, reflecting a stark departure from the so-called "Golden Age" of Freemasonry.[3]

However, what many have nostalgically called the Golden Age may be more aptly described as the "Art Deco Age" of Freemasonry—brilliant and grand in form but ultimately superficial in its adherence to the deeper speculative traditions that should define the Craft. The façade of high membership masked structural weaknesses, including a growing detachment from the fraternity's intellectual and spiritual heritage.

In Lodges across America, from grand halls in bustling cities to modest meeting rooms in rural towns, a concerning silence is growing. Chairs once filled with vibrant discussion now sit empty. Once a cornerstone of American social life, Freemasonry is now facing an existential threat. This is not merely an isolated issue but a nationwide trend affecting Masonry at every level.

Between 2002 and 2017, Grand Lodges across the United States faced substantial declines in membership. The smaller Masonic jurisdictions, which are more sensitive to demographic shifts, were

2   Masonic Service Association of North America, "U.S. Membership Statistics – Masonic Service Association of North America," 2023, https://msana.com/services/u-s-membership-statistics/.

3   MSANA.

4

particularly vulnerable. Medium, small, and tiny Grand Lodges have all reported significant drops, exacerbated by an inability to retain younger members.

This steady decline, with no clear indication of stabilization, is anticipated to continue for the foreseeable future. The Knights of the North, a collective of anonymous Freemasons, discuss these matters in great detail in *Laudable Pursuit II*. Projections suggest that by 2043, many Grand Lodges could see their numbers fall below levels required for independent operation.[4] Yet this isn't the first time Freemasonry has faced such a challenge. In the aftermath of the Anti-Masonic movement of the 1830s, the fraternity experienced sharp declines, but it emerged stronger, revitalizing its role in American life through reinvention and resilience. The difference today lies in a rapidly changing society, where technological advancements and shifting values are transforming the way people connect and find meaning.

Generational and Cultural Shifts

The sharp decline in Freemasonry's membership over the past century is rooted in profound generational and ideological shifts. The Baby Boomer generation largely rejected the institutions of their fathers, including Freemasonry, as part of the broader cultural upheavals of the 1960s and 1970s. For many Boomers, joining their fathers' Lodges symbolized an adherence to outdated norms, prompting a wholesale disengagement from fraternal organizations.

This rejection of authority and tradition coincided with the rise of postmodernism, which challenged modernist ideals like struc-

---

4   The Knights of the North, "Laudable Pursuit ii: Examining the Progress and Future of Regular Freemasonry in North America" (2019). https://theknightsofthenorth.org/wp-content/uploads/2019/06/Laudable-Pursuit-2.pdf.

ture and certainty, values that Freemasonry represents. For many Baby Boomers, joining such an institution would be seen as worship of the past rather than a step into the future.

Following this, Generation X did little to stem the decline. As a smaller demographic cohort, they never significantly contributed to Freemasonry's ranks. More importantly, their skepticism of institutions, born from an era of economic uncertainty and cultural fragmentation, kept them at arm's length from organizations like Freemasonry.

Millennials, in contrast, entered Freemasonry with curiosity. A noticeable number sought out the fraternity in search of mysticism, tradition, and community. However, many of them were met with a version of Freemasonry that had devolved into postmodern minimalism, its deeper philosophical and esoteric dimensions often reduced to practicalities. The rituals, once rich with allegorical and spiritual significance, felt hollow and detached from their original speculative meanings. As a result, many disillusioned Millennials left as quickly as they joined, realizing that Freemasonry no longer aligned with the mystical or intellectual journey they sought.

So now, as we hope to attract middle-aged Millennials and Generation Z, who are entering early adulthood, we may find that what they want is not what we're offering, but what we used to offer. What these men seek is not novelty, but a return to deeper connection, intellectual rigor, and the sense of community that was once Freemasonry's strength.

It is no welcome tiding that societal changes in the structure of family and community have exacerbated male isolation. As recent studies show, male loneliness is at an all-time high.[5] Many men today rely heavily on their romantic partners for emotional and social support—roles traditionally shared among male peers in fraternal and civic groups. In fact, it's becoming increasingly common for

5 Avrum Weiss, "The High Cost of Men's Loneliness," *Psychology Today*, November 21, 2021.

men to report having no close friends outside of their partners or immediate family, a stark contrast to previous generations when male bonding was integral to personal and social identity.[6]

Loneliness has severe mental and physical health impacts, contributing to issues like depression, cardiovascular disease, and even suicide, with men making up a significant portion of successful suicide cases. Research suggests that men who lack strong male friendships are more likely to face these challenges alone, without a support network to fall back on.[7] Men learn how to be men from other men, and in the absence of fathers or male role models, many young men struggle to find their place in the world. Without a sense of belonging or clear identity, they turn to online communities or become socially isolated.

The statistics paint a stark picture of male isolation in modern society. Yet amidst this crisis, some men are rediscovering traditional paths to brotherhood. Fraternal orders can provide "a sense of community and trust that I have never found anywhere else, that nothing is off-limits."[8] While contemporary society often lacks structured spaces for male bonding, Masonic lodges have emerged as what members describe as "oases of support and male camaraderie in a modern desert of political division."[9] These spaces offer what many men desperately seek: a place where vulnerability is met with understanding rather than judgment, and where mentorship occurs naturally through intergenerational connections.

6   Daniel A. Cox, "The State of American Friendship: Change, Challenges, and Loss," The Survey Center on American Life (blog), 2021.

7   Nick Norman, "Why So Many Men Feel Lonely Today," *Psychology Today*, 2023.

8   Allegra Rosenberg, "What If the Solution to Men's Loneliness Is . . . Freemasonry?" *Slate*, September 28, 2024, https://slate.com/life/2024/09/freemasons-lodges-conspiracies-membership-requirements.html.

9   Ibid.

In this context, Freemasonry stands as an institution uniquely positioned to be a balm on the rash on male isolation. As faith in traditional institutions wanes, Freemasonry offers a community that emphasizes moral development, intellectual engagement, and the kind of male mentorship that is increasingly hard to find elsewhere. The Craft's Speculative tradition—its teachings on self-improvement, wisdom, and the pursuit of light—could be precisely the kind of anchor young men are seeking in a chaotic, disorienting world.

Signs of Renewal

Historically, Freemasonry has proven remarkably adept at surviving crises, and, perhaps more impressively, not despite its members—but in many cases, because of them. From the Anti-Masonic movement of the 1830s to the membership slumps following the post-World War II boom, Freemasonry has continuously managed to dust itself off and return to its roots. Whether through an emphasis on education, charity, or spiritual introspection, the fraternity has always found a way to rebuild after nearly being left for dead.

But here's the thing: Freemasonry's greatest defense against decline has always been its ability to protect itself from the very people who claim to shepherd it. When faced with leadership that has forgotten its purpose, or rituals drained of meaning, Freemasonry steps in—quietly, subtly, and often subversively—to ensure that its real essence remains untouched.

William Preston knew this all too well. His famous words, while elegant on the surface, carry a hidden bite for those who care to look deeper:

> The lapse of time, the ruthless hand of ignorance, and the devastations of war have laid waste and destroyed many valuable monuments of antiquity. Even the temple of King Solomon, so

spacious and magnificent, and constructed by so many celebrated artists, was yet laid in ruin, and escaped not the unsparing ravages of barbarous force. Freemasonry, notwithstanding, has been able still to survive. The attentive ear receives the sound from the instructing tongue, and its sacred mysteries are safely lodged in the repository of faithful breasts. The tools and implements of architecture, symbols the most expressive, imprint on the memory wise and serious truths, and transmit unimpaired, through the succession of ages, the exquisitely incomparable tenets of this institution.[10]

There's a sly genius in Preston's words: Freemasonry survives because it adapts, but not in the way most people think. It doesn't twist itself to the whims of those who misunderstand it; instead, it buries its true essence deep, away from the careless hands of those who may misuse it. It survives not because of its leadership, but in spite of it, lodging its mysteries safely where they can't be corrupted—hidden in plain sight, waiting for those with the right kind of eyes and hearts to see it.

Freemasonry's survival through crisis, therefore, isn't just about bouncing back from external threats. It's about ensuring that the essence of the Craft remains unaltered, even if the outward form wobbles from time to time. And therein lies its true power: the ability to subvert its own decline by keeping the light burning, not for everyone, but for those who truly seek it.

Some Lodges are rising to this challenge. By emphasizing education and personal development, leveraging technology to connect members remotely, and focusing on impactful community service, these Lodges are rediscovering Freemasonry's philosophical and

10   William Preston, *Illustrations of Masonry: A Grand Gala in Honour of Free Masonry, Held at the Crown and Anchor Tavern, in the Strand* (London: Brother J. Williams, opposite St. Dunstan's Church, Fleet Street, 1772), 13–14.

symbolic roots. They are presenting the deeper mysteries of the Craft—its teachings on morality, self-reflection, and the quest for wisdom—in ways that appeal to today's generation of Masons and potential initiates.

Lodges that thrive in this changing landscape are those that emphasize the timeless aspects of Freemasonry: its intellectual rigor, spiritual exploration, and moral instruction. The fraternity's wealth of symbolism—from the working tools to the allegory of the Temple—offers powerful metaphors for self-improvement and community building. Younger men seeking to make sense of a rapidly changing world are often drawn to traditions that offer depth, meaning, and an opportunity for self-reflection.

Technology, often seen as a challenge to traditional fraternal life, can also be an asset. Online discussions and digital learning platforms provide opportunities for Freemasons to connect across distances and to engage with Masonic education in new ways. The post-COVID world has shown that these tools can enhance—but never replace—the in-person experience that is central to the Craft.

The task before us is not about reinventing the wheel; it's about rediscovering Freemasonry's core purpose and adapting it to the needs of the modern man. The strength of the Craft has always been in its ability to foster brotherhood and personal growth. By focusing on what made Freemasonry powerful in the first place, it can offer the moral and intellectual guidance that so many men are searching for in today's chaotic world.

The path forward is neither clear nor easy. It requires a willingness to evolve, to question long-held practices while remaining true to the core principles that have sustained the Craft for centuries. It demands a collective effort, much like the symbolism of the beehive—central to Masonic teachings—emphasizing industry, harmony, and community. Freemasonry, if it is to survive and thrive, must balance its rich heritage with the need to be responsive to the lives and values of today's men.

This renewal is not about abandoning Freemasonry's traditions but rather about rediscovering their relevance for a modern audience. The speculative nature of the Craft—the search for light, the building of character, and the pursuit of wisdom—remains as essential today as it was in the eighteenth century. But to keep the light burning, the Craft must find ways to make those eternal truths resonate in new and dynamic ways.

The story of Freemasonry's future is yet to be written. But one thing is clear: the next chapter in the History of Freemasonry will be crucial in determining whether this venerable institution will fade into obscurity or shine anew in the modern world. Like the beehive, Freemasonry must harness the industrious spirit of its members, working collectively to secure the future of the Craft. By embracing renewal and adaptation, Freemasonry can emerge not as a relic of the past but as a vibrant force for the future.

British historian Eric Hobsbawm describes Freemasonry as an "invented tradition of great symbolic force."[11] He said we invented our past. I say we should invent our future. As Dennis Gabor, the Nobel Prize-winning physicist, indicates:

> The future cannot be predicted, but futures can be invented. It was man's ability to invent which has made human society what it is. The mental processes of inventions are still mysterious. They are rational but not logical, that is to say, not deductive.[12]

As we look to the future, the lessons from Freemasonry's past can guide us toward renewal. The beehive, with its symbolism of harmony, industriousness, and unity, offers a model for how the Craft can thrive in the twenty-first century. By embracing both our traditions

---

11   Eric Hobsbawm and Terence Ranger, eds., *The Invention of Tradition* (Cambridge, UK: Cambridge University Press, 1992), 6.

12   Dennis Gabor, *Inventing the Future* (London: Secker & Warburg, 1963), 184–85.

and the need for adaptation, we can ensure that Freemasonry not only survives but flourishes. It is through this balance—honoring the past while evolving for the future—that we will prepare for the Quadricentennial, securing Freemasonry's place as a force for moral and spiritual improvement for generations to come.

The Road Ahead

It is time to actually set the Craft to labor. Lodges are facing financial strains as dues income shrinks. Historic Masonic buildings, once points of pride in their communities, have become burdens, with maintenance costs that smaller Lodges can no longer afford. For many jurisdictions, especially in rural areas, sustainability has become a looming concern. Some Grand Lodges, unable to justify the upkeep of multiple properties, have begun to consider consolidating Lodges or even closing some altogether.

But the membership crisis isn't just about numbers or financial sustainability. It's about the vibrancy of the Craft itself. Freemasonry has always thrived on personal connection, moral instruction, and the collective pursuit of higher knowledge. When those connections fray, the fraternity risks losing its unique role as a space where men of diverse backgrounds come together to improve themselves and their communities.

Freemasonry's future depends on our ability to adapt without compromising the deeper meanings and teachings that define the Craft. The trestleboard has always symbolized the designs and plans for future work. Now, it becomes the symbol for how we, as Masons, must take up the tools at our disposal—our history, traditions, and values—and use them to build a future that resonates with both modern Masons and those yet to come.

To the Mason, this recommends wise and serious meditation. Take a moment to reflect on the current state of your Lodge. Are your efforts focused more on increasing membership numbers, or are you prioritizing the depth and quality of the Masonic experience? As we see in many Lodges today, there is often a push for quantity—filling seats and initiating new members—but how often do we pause to consider if we're providing them with the rich intellectual and spiritual journey that Freemasonry promises?

Ask yourself:

> *Is your Lodge striking a balance between the practical aspects of operations—such as meetings, charity, and administration—and the Speculative, philosophical side of the Craft?*

> *Are the initiations and rituals being conducted with the care and reverence they deserve, or are they rushed and superficial?*

> *Are the teachings of the degrees truly resonating with the brethren, or do they feel more like formalities to get through?*

These are not new questions. As Dwight Smith so aptly observed in the 1960s, the fraternity's most pressing challenges often arise not from external pressures, but from within—from a lack of commitment to the meaningful experience Freemasonry can offer. What can you do to ensure that your Lodge thrives not just in numbers, but in the substance of its members' growth?

In reflecting on how to revitalize our Lodges, we turn to one of the most profound symbols in Masonic tradition: the beehive. Throughout this book, the beehive will serve as a guiding metaphor for how Freemasonry can reclaim its balance of practical work and spiritual depth. The beehive, emblematic of unity, industry, and harmony, perfectly encapsulates both the Operative and Speculative aspects of the Craft.

Just as each bee in the hive has a role that contributes to the overall harmony and productivity of the colony, so too must each Mason contribute to the same within the Lodge. The beehive teaches us that the practical tasks—like running the Lodge, maintaining relationships, and supporting charity—are essential, but so too are the speculative teachings: the pursuit of wisdom, self-improvement, and moral betterment.

The beauty of the beehive lies in its balance: every element works in service of a higher purpose. This symbol inspires us to foster an environment where practical efficiency and intellectual, spiritual growth can coexist. Freemasonry, like the beehive, thrives when all members work in unity, striving toward a common goal of personal and communal improvement.

PART
I

The Beehive
in Masonic
Tradition

1

The Sacred Hive: Origins and Evolution

THE BEEHIVE, a potent symbol across various cultures, has long been revered for its industriousness, harmony, and order. For Freemasonry, it represents both practical labor and speculative thought—principles deeply embedded in the Craft's traditions. As Masons, we are drawn to the beehive not just for its historical roots but for the profound lessons it offers us on how to build a collective society, while also seeking personal enlightenment.

The Bee in Ancient Egypt and the Classical World

Ancient Egyptians were known to revere insect life, such as the scarab, but the bee was also a symbol of divine kingship and unity. The bee symbolized Lower Egypt. The title 🐝 or "of the Sedge and the Bee" was bestowed upon Pharaohs, symbolizing their dominion over both Upper and Lower Egypt.[13] This union reflected the

13   Ronald J. Leprohon, *The Great Name: Ancient Egyptian Royal*

18

seamless cooperation of a society organized under a single divine authority, much like the harmonious structure of a beehive.

For the Egyptians, bees were believed to have been born from the tears of Ra, the sun god, further intertwining them with themes of immortality and divine purpose.[14] The structured, efficient life of the hive mirrored the pharaoh's role—ensuring balance and prosperity, much like our Masonic obligations to society and each other. Here, we see the first threads of the beehive's relevance to Freemasonry: an emblem of harmony and unity, serving a higher purpose.

Beyond its practical significance, the beehive held profound spiritual meaning in ancient Greece. Bees were viewed as intermediaries between the human and divine realms, symbolizing the soul's immortality and its connection to higher forces. This spiritual association is evident in the writings of Porphyry, who described bees as "nymphs, that are souls."[15] This connection between bees and the soul was further emphasized through their association with the Greek mysteries, such as the Oracle of Trophonius, where a swarm of bees guided seekers to the sacred site.

The bee's ability to produce honey, a substance believed to have divine properties, further solidified its sacred status. The beehive, therefore, represented not only order and industry, but also a conduit to the divine and a symbol of the soul's journey and potential for immortality. This multifaceted symbolism underscores the profound reverence that ancient Greeks held for these creatures and their connection to the mysteries of life and the cosmos.

In ancient Rome, the beehive was admired for its representation of order and collective labor. This is evident in the writings of

Titulary (Society of Biblical Lit, 2013).

14   Kirsten Traynor, "The Tears of Re: Beekeeping in Ancient Egypt," *American Entomologist* 62, no. 3 (2016): 194–96.

15   George W. Bullamore, "The Beehive and Freemasonry," *Ars Quatuor Coronatorum* 36 (1923): 225.

Seneca, who compared the bee-state to a well-structured human monarchy. He highlighted the bees' organized society, with the king (queen bee in reality) at the center, overseeing the workers and maintaining order within the hive.[16] This orderly structure, where each bee had a specific role and contributed to the collective good, resonated with the Roman appreciation for discipline and a well-organized society.

Furthermore, the Romans recognized the beehive as a symbol of industriousness and practical benefits. They practiced beekeeping on a large scale, recognizing the value of honey and wax.[17] The industry surrounding beekeeping, with its organized hives, transportation of bees for better foraging, and the production of various honey-based products, reflects the Roman appreciation for the practical applications of a well-coordinated collective effort.

British Traditions and Sacred Connections

Beekeeping has deep roots in the British Isles, dating back to ancient times. The abundance of honey, used for mead production and as a sweetener, made beekeeping essential to daily life.[18] This long-standing tradition suggests that the beehive, as a physical representation of this practice, would have held a place of significance within British culture.

Bees are associated with the sacred in the British Isles, particularly through stories of saints and their miraculous interactions with these creatures. The belief that bees originated in Paradise, explicitly mentioned in Irish Brehon Laws, cemented their sacred status. The use of beeswax in church rituals, as it "was the only

---

16   Hilda M. Ransome, *The Sacred Bee in Ancient Times and Folklore* (London: George Allen & Unwin, 1937), 87.

17   Ransome, *The Sacred Bee*, 88.

18   Ransome, *The Sacred Bee*, 189.

substance worthy to make the candles for the sacred mass," further underscores this connection.[19] This sacred association imbues the beehive with a spiritual dimension, hinting at a deeper meaning beyond its practical function.

In British folklore, the belief in "bee-souls" offers a fascinating perspective, elevating bees beyond their role as mere messengers of the divine. Rather, these creatures were thought to embody souls, capable of moving between the physical and spiritual realms—a metaphor that resonates deeply with Masonic teachings.

For example, stories from Lincolnshire, Sutherlandshire, and Ross-shire tell of souls temporarily taking the form of bees. In one notable Lincolnshire tale, a man's soul, trapped in the form of a bee, is stuck within a hole. Only when the bee is released does the man awaken from his troubled sleep.[20] Such accounts reflect the belief that bees could serve as vessels for the soul's journey, connecting the earthly and the ethereal.

This mystical view extended to beliefs surrounding witchcraft. In parts of Scotland, witches were thought to transform into bees, carrying poison and practicing harmful magic.[21] This duality—bees as both symbols of life and agents of destruction—mirrors the delicate balance Masons strive for in their moral and spiritual work, seeking the good while guarding against the corrupting forces of the profane.

A particularly poignant tradition, "telling the bees," points to the bee's spiritual significance. Across England, Wales, and Scotland, it was customary to inform the bees of significant events, especially deaths, to prevent their departure or demise. The belief was that bees, intertwined with the souls of the dead, must be honored with this ritual to maintain harmony.[22] This practice subtly points to the

19   Ransome, *The Sacred Bee*, 196.
20   Ransome, *The Sacred Bee*, 222.
21   Ransome, *The Sacred Bee*, 224.
22   Ransome, *The Sacred Bee*, 221–22.

Masonic idea of continuity between life and death, reinforcing the beehive as a symbol of immortality.

Further evidence of the bees' divine association appears in the belief that they participated in the birth of Christ. In places like Northumberland, Cumberland, and Yorkshire, it was said that bees hummed a "Christmas hymn" at midnight on Christmas Eve.[23] This symbolism of bees heralding sacred moments reflects their revered status as creatures bridging the human and divine.

The complex relationship between bees, souls, and the divine in British folklore adds rich layers to our understanding of the beehive in Freemasonry. Much like the immortal soul, bees are timeless workers of creation, building their hive as Masons labor to perfect themselves and their communities. In this light, the beehive stands as a powerful symbol of industriousness, immortality, and the soul's connection to the divine—a reminder that, through unity and purpose, we transcend the material world and partake in the eternal.

Society in Miniature

Throughout history, the beehive has been a powerful metaphor for human society, a notion embraced both in ancient Rome and the British Isles. Shakespeare himself captured this vision in his famous lines, likening the beehive to "a peopled kingdom," where each bee plays its designated role for the collective good.[24] This imagery of the hive as a well-ordered, harmonious society mirrors the Masonic ideal, where every brother, like the bee, contributes to the greater whole.

Within the Lodge, the beehive serves as a symbol of unity, industriousness, and purpose. Just as each bee has a distinct role in maintaining the hive's structure, Masons work together to build

23   Ransome, *The Sacred Bee*, 229.
24   William Shakespeare, *King Henry V*, ed. Walter J. Black (New York: Walter J. Black, 1937), 1.2.197.

their moral and spiritual edifice, fulfilling their duties with diligence and mutual respect. The beehive's organization reflects the Masonic emphasis on order, hierarchy, and collective effort, reminding us that through cooperation and shared purpose, we create something greater than ourselves.

Early Masonic Adoptions

Freemasonry's embrace of the beehive builds upon ancient traditions, but with a distinctly speculative twist. By the eighteenth century, the beehive had firmly taken its place in Masonic symbolism, representing not just physical labor, but also the intellectual and moral work that every Mason is called to pursue. The beehive came to symbolize industry, unity, and the shared effort of building not only physical structures, but also a more enlightened and virtuous self.

Several key historical examples demonstrate the beehive's growing prominence in Masonic iconography:

- 1744: A silver medal commemorating Jonathan of the Pillar at Brunswick features bees on its reverse side, showcasing an early link between the bee and Masonic themes.
- 1755: Two Masonic charts, one held by the Quatuor Coronati Lodge and another in Ipswich, display five beehives arranged on a triangular stand, highlighting the symbol's connection to Masonic teachings [see Fig. 1].
- 1771: The petition submitted by De Vignoles and others to the Grand Lodge concerning Lodge L'Immortalitè de l'Ordre features two representations of the beehive on its cover, reinforcing the bee's role in Masonic identity.
- 1785 (or later): Two lodge banners belonging to True Blue Nº 253 in Carrickfergus depict the beehive. Though the older banner cannot be dated before 1785, this marks another signi-

ficant moment in the symbol's rise.

- 1793: A copper token engraved with the beehive and the motto "Industry has its sure reward" shows the broader societal appeal of this symbol in the late eighteenth century, extending even beyond Freemasonry.
- 1801: An Irish Knights Templar certificate includes a beehive illustration in its right-hand margin, further evidence of the symbol's penetration into Masonic visual language.

Another early reference comes from Jonathan Swift's *A Letter from the Grand Mistress*, believed to have been published between 1727 and 1730.[25] Though satirical in nature, Swift's essay suggests that the bee was already circulating within Masonic circles during this period, further cementing its relevance.[26]

While the precise timeline for the bee's adoption into Masonic symbolism remains unclear, these historical examples offer a compelling glimpse into the beehive's enduring presence across various periods and regions.

Fig. 1. Detail from William Tringham's highly symbolic *The Mysteries that here are Shown are only to a Mason known*, 1755. Three bees hover over five hives.

What is evident, however, is that the beehive evolved in parallel with Freemasonry, becoming a timeless representation of industry, fraternity, and the moral refinement that every Mason strives to achieve.

Yet the beehive's symbolism extends beyond mere indus-

---

25 Bullamore, "The Beehive and Freemasonry," 220.

26 Shawn Eyer, "The Beehive and the Stock of Knowledge," *Philalethes: The Journal of Masonic Research & Letters* 63, no. 1 (2010): 36.

triousness. It also conveys diligence and a protective posture, emblematic of the care Masons must take to preserve the integrity of the Craft. To early Masons, the beehive likely represented not just the physical Lodge, but Lodge culture itself—a symbol of the collective spirit and unity within the brotherhood.[27] The beehive reflects a readiness to defend these ideals, much like bees protect their hive from threats.

In this way, the beehive served as a reminder that Masons must not only labor for self-improvement and the betterment of society, but also remain vigilant in safeguarding the core values and traditions that make Freemasonry a unique and enduring institution.

The Lessons of the Beehive

Within the Craft, the beehive serves as an essential model for balancing both practical and spiritual work—just as the guilds balanced the physical construction of cathedrals with the pursuit of personal enlightenment. In the Lodge, the beehive represents more than a bustling society; it embodies the principle of unity through diversity. Each bee, much like each Mason, has a vital role in the success of the hive.

Whether through acts of charity or the deepening of philosophical understanding, the harmony of the Lodge depends on every member's efforts. Moreover, the beehive emphasizes the equality of this labor. Just as all bees are equal in their pursuit of the hive's success, so too are Masons equal in their pursuit of wisdom and moral refinement.

Freemasonry's adoption of the beehive reflects a union of ancient ideas of kingship and labor with the fraternity's focus on intellectual and moral development. It reminds us that, like bees, we are tasked with both practical work and the continuous refinement of our cha-

27 Eyer, "The Beehive and the Stock of Knowledge," 37.

racter. The beehive teaches that our labor is twofold: we must work for the benefit of others while also striving for personal growth.

Industriousness, Harmony, and the Balance of Labor

The beehive is a potent symbol in Freemasonry, representing the virtues of industriousness, harmonious cooperation, and the balance between Operative and Speculative labor. Its symbolism urges us to blend practical action with introspective wisdom, creating a society built on mutual effort and self-improvement.

The hive, with its tireless activity, serves as a constant reminder of the Mason's duty to be industrious in all aspects of life. This industriousness extends beyond physical labor, encompassing intellectual and spiritual pursuits as well. The beehive signifies Industry, Perseverance, and Diligence, values that every Mason should embrace. Just as bees constantly strive to gather nectar and build their hive, Masons are called to work tirelessly toward personal and collective goals, contributing to the betterment of themselves and society.

The beehive also exemplifies the principles of harmony and cooperation, reflecting the structure of the Lodge. In the hive, each bee plays a vital role, working in unison with others to achieve a common goal. This hierarchical yet harmonious society mirrors the Lodge, where members from diverse backgrounds and degrees collaborate, each offering unique talents and perspectives for the benefit of the whole.

As Shakespeare famously wrote in *Henry v*, the bees "have a king, and officers of sorts" all working together to the same end.[28] In this way, the beehive teaches that individual effort, when coordinated within a structured framework, results in something far greater than the sum of its parts.

28 William Shakespeare, *King Henry V*, ed. Walter J. Black (New York: Walter J. Black, 1937), 1.2.198.

Beyond Industry: The Deeper Symbolism

While the association of the beehive with industriousness is well known, its symbolism in Freemasonry holds deeper meaning. In fact, confusion regarding the symbol created uncertainty as to whether it belonged to the first degree or the third; its association with the third degree hinting at a more esoteric dimension.[29] In ancient cultures and mystery traditions, the bee was often linked with divinity, immortality, and the soul, adding layers of spiritual significance to its Masonic role.

The beehive has also been connected to the essence of the Lodge itself. As early as the eighteenth century, Lodges were sometimes referred to as "Hives of Free-Masons," indicating that the beehive represents not just individual virtues but the collective spirit and purpose of Freemasonry.[30] It stands as a symbol of the brotherhood's shared effort, unity, and determination to build a better society.

Over time, the beehive's symbolism may have evolved, with "Industry" becoming the dominant association and leading to confusion about whether it was more strongly associated with the first degree or the third. Yet, the beehive's deeper meaning remains: it is a reminder that true labor encompasses both hands and mind, practical effort and intellectual reflection.

The beehive is one of Freemasonry's most powerful and multifaceted symbols. It encapsulates the core values of industriousness, harmony, and the pursuit of knowledge, reminding Masons that their work must involve both physical and intellectual effort. By embodying the bee's tireless dedication to the collective good, Masons can build not only a stronger Lodge but also a more enlightened and virtuous society.

---

29   Bullamore, "The Beehive and Freemasonry," 231.
30   Eyer, "The Beehive and the Stock of Knowledge," 36.

2

The Evolution and Decline of the Beehive Symbol

T HE BEEHIVE HAS ENJOYED a rich history in Freemasonry, representing industry, cooperation, and the importance of working together for the common good. However, its prominence has varied across different regions and periods, particularly after the formation of the United Grand Lodge of England in 1813.

Post-1813 Transformations

Following the unification of the UGLE in 1813, the beehive symbol began to fade from use in English Freemasonry. Several factors contributed to this decline including standardization, political tensions, and popular culture.

The push for standardized rituals and tracing boards after the Union significantly impacted the symbolism used in English lodges. As uniformity became a priority, symbols that were once diverse in meaning and interpretation, like the beehive, were gradually phased out. The beehive, while prevalent in some regions, was not universally recognized across all lodges, and its removal from standardized tracing boards contributed to its decline.

Political and Cultural Influences

The beehive's association with Jacobite symbolism after the Battle of Culloden in 1746 further complicated its place in Freemasonry. For the Jacobites, the bee and beehive represented "The Return of the Soul," a hopeful allusion to the restoration of the Stuart line.[31] However, with the defeat of the Jacobite cause and its subsequent persecution, the political implications of this symbol made it less desirable within mainstream Freemasonry, which sought to distance itself from divisive political movements.

Dr. Isaac Watts's popular moral song, *How doth the little busy bee* (published in 1720), also played a role in shaping the perception of the beehive in Freemasonry.

> How doth the little busy bee
> Improve each shining hour,
> And gather honey all the day
> From every opening flower!

It is clear by the popularity of this song that the association between the industriousness of the bees and a pure morality is well-established by this time. A later verse states:

31   Bullamore, "The Beehive and Freemasonry," 233.

In works of labor or of skill,
I would be busy too;
For Satan finds some mischief still
For idle hands to do.[32]

As this interpretation took root, the beehive's broader symbolism—particularly its association with spiritual and moral improvement in the third degree—was overshadowed by its new role as a symbol of labor and industriousness for new initiates. This shift in focus contributed to the beehive's relocation from the third to the first degree and its gradual decline in prominence.[33]

Regional Variations

Despite its decline in the broader English Masonic tradition, the beehive symbol survived in certain lodges, such as the Royal Cumberland Lodge № 41 in Bath. This lodge retained the beehive symbol in its rituals, emphasizing the virtues of industriousness and mutual aid among its members. For example, their eighteenth century rituals describe:

> The beehive teaches us that as we are born into the world rational and intelligent beings, so ought we also to be industrious ones, and not stand idly by or gaze with listless indifference on even the meanest of our fellow creatures in a state of distress if it is in our power to help them without detriment to ourselves or our connections; the constant practice of this virtue is enjoined on all created beings, from the highest seraph in heaven to the meanest

32 Isaac Watts, *Divine Songs Attempted in Easy Language for the Use of Children*. 2nd ed. (London: Printed for M. Lawrence at the Angel in the Poultry, 1716), 29.
33 Bullamore, "The Beehive and Freemasonry," 231.

reptile that crawls in the dust.[34]

The persistence of the beehive in such lodges suggests a continued appreciation for its traditional values, even as broader trends moved away from these symbols.

American Continuity

In contrast to its decline in England, the beehive remained a prominent symbol in American Freemasonry. It continued to represent industriousness, cooperation, and the avoidance of idleness, aligning well with the values of the burgeoning American society.

The first known printing of the familiar beehive lecture appeared in Thomas Smith Webb's *The Freemason's Monitor, or Illustrations of Masonry in Two Parts*. This important text likely drew upon earlier rituals, such as those used by the Royal Cumberland Lodge № 41 in Bath. In it, Webb explains:

> The Bee-Hive is an emblem of industry, and recommends the practice of that virtue to all created beings, from the highest seraph in heaven, to the lowest reptile of the dust. It teaches us, that as we came into the world rational and intelligent beings, so we should ever be industrious ones; never sitting down contented while our fellow-creatures around us are in want, when it is in our power to relieve them, without inconvenience to ourselves.[35]

The Freemason's Monitor, Webb's adaptation of Preston's system, has become a cornerstone of Masonic practice in the United States.

---

34   Bullamore, "The Beehive and Freemasonry," 222.

35   Thomas Smith Webb, *The Freemason's Monitor; or, Illustrations of Masonry: In Two Parts* (New York: Printed by Southwick and Crooker No. 354, Water-Street, 1802), 77–78.

Within this ritual, the beehive prominently appears in the third degree, serving as a powerful reminder to Masons of the virtues of hard work, collaboration, and the necessity of active participation in the Lodge. Just as each bee contributes to the survival and prosperity of the hive, so too must every Mason contribute his labor and support to ensure the success of the Lodge and the welfare of his community.

In American Masonic rituals, the beehive also warns against intellectual and moral complacency. It emphasizes the responsibility of each brother to contribute meaningfully, both in thought and action, to the collective good. The bees' harmonious labor, producing something far greater than any one individual could achieve alone, reflects the collaborative spirit expected within the Lodge. This symbolism aligns perfectly with the American ethos of self-improvement and communal responsibility, reinforcing the idea that a Mason's work—whether physical, intellectual, or spiritual—must always serve a higher, nobler purpose.

As we have seen, the beehive's symbolism in Freemasonry is deeply rooted in the virtues of industry, collaboration, and moral responsibility—echoing the collective labor of bees in their hive. Yet beyond these immediate lessons lies a more profound teaching for the Craft. The beehive serves not only as a model for individual conduct but as a blueprint for how Freemasonry itself can thrive and evolve.

This imagining of the beehive as a model for planning, building, and renewal hints at how Freemasonry can draw inspiration from its timeless symbol to shape its future. The beehive is a blueprint for the Craft. It can lay the foundation for unity, adaptation, and lasting success.

PART
II

*The Beehive
as a Blueprint*

3

Masonic Renewal
through Industry
and Harmony

A S SHAWN EYER SAID, "perhaps a better way to express it is that the Beehive represents an ideal Lodge culture. After all, bees do what good Masons ought to do: they build their habitation according to the rules of geometry, they guard it from intrusion, they labor in union, they maintain order, they gather what is scattered, and within the confines of their temple, transform it into nourishment."[36]

There is eighteenth-century evidence evidence to support this.

---

36 Shawn Eyer, "The Beehive and the Stock of Knowledge," *Philalethes: The Journal of Masonic Research & Letters* 63 (2010): 37.

Christopher Smart, the English poet of some renown, wrote a 1762 Masonic song titled "A Mason is Great and Respected" in which he praises the industriousness and excellence of the "flower of the swarm." Smart demonstrates the Masonic values of diligence, productivity, and individual responsibility.

SONG by Brother C. Smart, A.M.
Tune, Ye frolicksome Sparks of the Game.

A MASON is great and respected,
Tho' Cavillers wrangle and mock;
His Plan is in Wisdom projected,
His Edifice built on a Rock.
Cho. The Attempts of his Foes miscarry,
—And ever in vain are found;
Or so wide, that they need no Parry,
Or so weak, that they make no Wound.

GOOD-NATURE's an Englishman's Merit,
A Title all Britons desire;
But We claim the Name and the Spirit,
From the CORNER-STONE up to the SPIRE.
Cho. The Attempts of our Foes miscarry, &c.

Tho' often decry'd and derided,
No Tyrant our Freedom controuls,
With us mighty MONARCHS have sided,
And EMP'ROR's are writ in our ROLLS.
Cho. The Attempts of our Foes miscarry, &c.

Then fill up the Glass and be funny,
Attend to due METHOD and FORM;
The Bee that can make the most Honey,

Is fairly the Flow'r of the Swarm.

Cho. The Attempts of our Foes miscarry, &c.[37]

Physical and Intellectual Work

Christopher Smart's 1762 Masonic song, set to the tune of "Ye frol-icksome Sparks of the Game," (Fig. 2) offers a vivid celebration of the values that the beehive symbolizes within Freemasonry. His verse, with its emphasis on industriousness and the triumph of Masonic virtues over opposition, aligns perfectly with the beehive as a metaphor for productive labor, both physical and intellectual, within the Lodge.

True greatness and respect are built upon a foundation of wisdom and diligent work. The imagery of the Lodge as an edi-fice "built on a Rock" reminds of the stability and resilience of the beehive, where each contributes to the strength and permanence of the whole. The refrain, "The Attempts of our Foes miscarry," cements the idea that no external forces can destabilize a structure founded on the principles of wisdom and labor.

Particularly striking is Smart's reference to the "flower of the swarm," which he uses to describe the bee that produces the most honey. This phrase encapsulates the essence of Masonic indus-triousness—where the most dedicated and productive members of the Lodge are celebrated not merely for their labor, but for the quality and sweetness of what they produce. Smart uses the beehive as a symbol of productive labor within Freemasonry. Just as bees work tirelessly to produce honey, Masons are encouraged to contribute to their Lodge and community, creating not just physical works but also fostering intellectual and spiritual growth—the honey of the hive.

37   [Anon], *A Defence of Free-Masonry, As Practiced in the Regular Lodges, Both Foreign and Domestic, Under the Constitution of the English Grand-Master* (London: Flexney and Hood, 1765), 64.

A Mason Is Great and Respected

Christopher Smart (1722–1771)

1. A Ma - son is great and re - spect - ed, Tho
2. Tho' of - ten de - cry'd and de - rid - ed, No

Cav - il - lers wran - gle and mock; His
ty - rant our Free - dom con - trols, With

Plan is in Wis - dom proj - ect - ed, His
us might - y Mon - archs have fid - ed, and

ed - i - fice built on a Rock. Good-
Em - p'rors are writ in our Rolls. Then

Na - ture's an Eng - lish - man's Mer - it, A
fill up the Glass and be fun - ny, At -

Ti - tle all Brit - ons de - sire; But
tend to due Meth - od and Form; The

We claim the Name and the Spir - it, From the
Bee that can make the most Hon - ey, Is____

Fig. 2. A Mason is Great and Respected,
by Bro. Christopher Smart, 1765.

Cor - ner - Stone up to the Spire.
fair - ly the flow'r of the swarm.

Refrain

The At - tempts of our Foes mis - car - ry, And
ev - er in vain are found; Or so
wide, that they need __ no Par - ry, Or
so weak, that they make no Wound.

1765

Beyond its representation of physical labor, the beehive also symbolizes the sweetness of wisdom that comes from intellectual and spiritual effort. In the Masonic tradition, honey represents the fruits of this labor—the knowledge, insight, and moral understanding that are cultivated through the collective efforts of the Lodge. Just as bees gather nectar to produce honey, Masons gather knowledge and experience, distilling it into wisdom that benefits the entire community.

The Lodge, seen as a hive, is where this collective wisdom is produced. Each Mason contributes his unique skills, experiences, and insights, much like individual bees contribute to the creation of honey. The "flower of the swarm" is not just the most industrious bee, but also the one whose efforts yield the sweetest results—an apt metaphor for the Mason who diligently seeks and imparts wisdom.

Christopher Smart's choice to visualize the "great and respected" Mason within the context of the beehive, strengthens the argument that productive labor is at the heart of Masonic work. Whether it is through the construction of physical edifices, the crafting of intellectual pursuits, or the nurturing of spiritual growth, the beehive serves as a powerful symbol of how individual contributions lead to collective success. The sweetness of honey, or wisdom, produced in this process is what truly enriches the Lodge and its members, ensuring that the efforts of the Masonic "swarm" are both meaningful and enduring.

The Warning of the Drones

The enduring Masonic legacy of the beehive emphasizes industriousness, particularly in the intellectual and spiritual domains. While practical labor is important, the true emphasis is on the continuous pursuit of knowledge and self-improvement as essential aspects of Masonic duty. This industriousness is not merely about keeping busy but about actively contributing to the useful knowledge and enduring intellectual legacy of the community. More specifically:

> Thus was man formed for social and active life, the noblest part of the work of God; and he that will so demean himself as not to be endeavoring to add to the common stock of knowledge and understanding, may be deemed a drone in the hive of nature, a useless member of society, and unworthy of our protection as Masons.[38]

Consequences of Inaction

The natural process of drone expulsion within a hive serves as a powerful metaphor for the principles of industriousness and accountability in Freemasonry. This event, occurring during autumn or when resources become scarce, highlights the beehive's efficiency and the importance of contribution to the collective well-being.

Drones, the male bees in a colony, have a singular purpose: to mate with the queen bee. Unlike worker bees, drones do not engage in hive-building, honey production, or any other tasks that support the hive's daily functioning. Their role is vital yet limited, with their entire existence centered on the reproductive success of the colony.

For the drone, mating is a fatal act. After fulfilling their sole purpose, they die, leaving behind those who have not yet mated. As winter approaches, any remaining drones are essentially surplus to the needs of the hive, having failed to fulfill their primary function.

It falls to the worker bees, the diligent laborers of the hive, to ensure the colony's survival through the harsh winter months. These worker bees take on the task of expelling the drones. Worker bees

---

38 Thomas Smith Webb, *The Freemason's Monitor; or, Illustrations of Masonry: In Two Parts* (New York: Printed by Southwick and Crooker No. 354, Water-Street, 1802), 78.

physically remove the drones from the hive, a necessary action to conserve resources for the colony's productive members.[39]

Once expelled, the drones, unable to forage or survive independently, soon succumb to the cold. Their expulsion, while harsh, is a pragmatic decision that ensures the survival of the hive by prioritizing those who contribute to its well-being.

The expulsion of drones serves as a solemn illustration of nature's efficiency and pragmatism—principles that resonate deeply within Masonic philosophy. Just as the beehive cannot sustain members who do not contribute, so too does Freemasonry emphasize the importance of active participation. Masons who fail to contribute to the fraternity and its ideals may find themselves similarly marginalized, a reminder that the Craft values the efforts and dedication of each member.

This should immediately remind us of the concept of "False Brethren," explained by so many early Masonic authors.[40] Unworthy men infiltrating the noble ranks of our fraternity is not a novel concern, but one that has long troubled the brethren who truly understand the essence of Masonry. While our doors are open to those who seek light, not all who enter are prepared to receive it in its fullness, nor are all capable of embodying the virtues we hold so dear.

The Masonic institution, being composed of men with varying dispositions and capacities, cannot escape the inevitable inclusion of some who fail to grasp its luminosity. Even among the most select of assemblies, imperfections must be tolerated. When addressing the Grand Lodge of Scotland in 1763, David Erskine Baker made the

39 Eyer, "The Beehive and the Stock of Knowledge," 36.
40 Christopher B. Murphy, "Assessing Authentic Lodge Culture: Moving Beyond the Tavern Myth," in *Exploring Early Grand Lodge Freemasonry: Studies in Honor of the Tricentennial of the Establishment of the Grand Lodge of England*, ed. Christopher B. Murphy and Shawn Eyer (Washington, D.C.: Plumbstone, 2017), 409–15.

argument that even among the twelve chosen by the Christian Master, one was found to be a betrayer.[41] Such is the human condition that no society, however vigilant, can be entirely free from error.

William Preston himself, a man of discerning judgment, lamented the overextension of Masonic privileges, observing that our Craft had, at times, been too liberal in bestowing its honors. When men of low character or deficient understanding are admitted, they tarnish the reputation of the fraternity and impede its true mission.[42]

The existence of False Brethren, therefore, is not just a blemish on the record of our fraternity but a call to greater vigilance and discernment. It is a duty incumbent upon every true Mason to guard the sanctity of our Craft, ensuring that only those who are sincerely dedicated to its ideals are admitted into its mysteries. By doing so, we safeguard Freemasonry from the insidious influence of those who would distort its teachings for personal gain or out of sheer misunderstanding. In this way, we must be ever watchful over the admission of candidates, to the end that the fraternity may continue to be a beacon of virtue and wisdom in a world often overshadowed by ignorance and vice.

The metaphor of drone expulsion highlights the necessity of each Mason's commitment to the collective goals of the Lodge. The worker bees' actions underscore the value of contributing to the greater good, and the fate of the drones serves as a cautionary tale

41 David Erskine Baker, *An Oration in Honour of Free-Masonry. Delivered before the Honourable and Worshipful the Grand Lodge of Scotland. 30th November, 1763. Being St. Andrew's Day.* (Edinburgh, 1763), 13–14.

42 Christopher B. Murphy, "Assessing Authentic Lodge Culture: Moving Beyond the Tavern Myth," in *Exploring Early Grand Lodge Freemasonry: Studies in Honor of the Tricentennial of the Establishment of the Grand Lodge of England*, ed. Christopher B. Murphy and Shawn Eyer (Washington, D.C.: Plumbstone, 2017), 410.

about the consequences of idleness and non-participation.

Shawn Eyer connects intellectual laziness with the symbol of the drone in the beehive. Just as drones don't contribute to the building or sustenance of the hive, intellectually lazy Freemasons fail to contribute to the "common stock of knowledge and understanding" within their Lodges.[43] This means actively engaging with the intellectual and philosophical dimensions of Freemasonry.

The beehive continues to teach that the strength of the Fraternity is the active and meaningful engagement of all its members. There is a purposeful parallel to be drawn between the expulsion of drones and the Masonic directive to be intellectually active. As drones that do not contribute to the hive are expelled, Masons who fail to engage in self-improvement and lodge work are considered "useless members of society," "unworthy of our protection," and likened to "drones in the hive of nature."[44] Let there be no misunderstanding regarding the importance of continuous learning and active participation in Masonic life.

Practical and Speculative Harmony

To address this, we must focus on the use of our own lexicon. Freemasons have always understood that our Ancient Brethren worked on the physical world, but also on the individual self. William Preston refers to these by the denominations "Operative" and "Speculative" and states:

> By [Operative Masonry], we allude to the useful rules of architecture, whence a structure derives figure, strength and beauty;

43   Eyer, "The Beehive and the Stock of Knowledge," 37.
44   Thomas Smith Webb, *The Freemason's Monitor; or, Illustrations of Masonry: In Two Parts* (New York: Printed by Southwick and Crooker No. 354, Water-Street, 1802), 78.

and whence results due proportion and a just correspondence in all its parts…Operative masonry furnishes us with dwellings and convenient shelters from the vicissitudes and the inclemencies of seasons. It displays human wisdom in a proper arrangement of materials, and demonstrates that a fund of science and industry is implanted in the rational species for the most wise, salutary, and beneficent purposes….

By [Speculative Masonry], we learn to subdue the passions, act upon the square, keep a tongue of good report, maintain secrecy, and practice charity. Speculative masonry is so much interwoven with religion, as to lay us under the strongest obligations to pay to the Deity that rational homage, which at once constitutes the duty and happiness of mankind. It leads the contemplative to view with reverence and admiration the glorious works of the creation, and inspires them with the most exalted ideas of the perfections of the great Creator.[45]

Contemporary Masons are familiar with this reference to Operative Masonry as "rules of architecture," but this reference was intended to dovetail with Speculative Masonry which similarly inculcates the "rules of philosophy." This is an important use of terminology, because "by both united, the art is formed"—the art, of course, being *The Royal Art*, or the Ancient and Gentle Craft.[46]

It is clear that Preston understood the denominations to be two sides of the same coin intimately inseparable. Contemporary Masons are often informed that our pursuit is Speculative Masonry only, but our Ancient Brethren engaged in both. This seems to be a late addition to our lexicon. This idea can be seen with the Emulation Work in the 1820s, but it is not of the early Craft. In

45   Preston, *Illustrations of Masonry: A Grand Gala in Honour of Free Masonry, Held at the Crown and Anchor Tavern, in the Strand,* 12–13.

46   Colin F. W. Dyer, *William Preston and His Work* (Shepperton, UK: Lewis Masonic, 1987), 235

46

fact, it would be unsurprising if at least some of these rituals were unknowingly quoting Albert Mackey from the 1860s, almost a century after Preston's remarks:

> We work, it is true, in speculative Masonry only, but our ancient brethren wrought in both Operative and speculative; and it is now well understood that the two branches are widely apart in design and in character—the one a mere useful art, intended for the protection and convenience of man and the gratification of his physical wants, the other a profound science, entering into abstruse investigations of the soul and a future existence, and originating in the craving need of humanity to know something that is above and beyond the mere outward life that surrounds us with its gross atmosphere here below. Indeed, the only bond or link that unites speculative and Operative Masonry is the symbolism that belongs altogether to the former, but which, throughout its whole extent, is derived from the latter.[47]

Not only is this thought a century removed from Preston, but it seems to miss the author's intent. Speculative masonry is not reading minutes, nitpicking over minutiae, and eating canned green beans, while bellyaching about 'kids these days.' I suggest that in the twenty-first century, the *Operative* work of the Lodge has morphed into the practical, logistical tasks of running a modern organization—things like committee meetings, fundraising, and charitable events—whereas the *speculative* work, the pursuit of philosophy, mysticism, and deeper spiritual inquiry, has taken a backseat. In a sense, we've flipped Mackey's dichotomy. Instead of distinguishing sharply between speculative (intellectual) and Operative (practical) Masonry, it seems the Fraternity has coalesced almost entirely

47 Albert G. Mackey, *The Symbolism Of Freemasonry: Illustrating and Explaining its Science and Philosophy, its Legends, Myths, and Symbols* (New York: Clark and Maynard, 1869), 77–78.

toward operational matters, leaving the speculative dimensions at best underexplored or diminished.

The "New" Operative Lodge

At the time of this printing, too much of Freemasonry's time is spent on administrative tasks, logistical planning, and charitable endeavors. These are certainly noble pursuits, but they can often feel like the "new" Operative masonry—a kind of project management that deals with the day-to-day functioning of the Lodge. In many cases, floorwork, fundraisers, and community service are what define the public face of the Lodge. This has shifted the focus away from the speculative traditions that once captivated men like Preston and his contemporaries.

What's striking about this is that modern Freemasonry seems to be caught in a loop of doing rather than being. The Lodge has become a place where the execution of tasks (the profane kind) takes priority, often crowding out the space for intellectual, philosophical, or esoteric reflection.

We must finally acknowledge the twentieth century's war on true speculative work—philosophical inquiry, mysticism, and esoteric practice. In most Lodges, there is little time devoted to the study of metaphysics, symbolism, or the deeper meanings behind Masonic rituals. This is unfortunate, given that Freemasonry originally emerged as a speculative system precisely to engage with these higher forms of knowledge. Speculative Masonry is about refining the inner temple, seeking wisdom, and aligning with the Divine principles that the Craft tools symbolically represent.[48]

In our world, there is a hunger for meaning in the face of increasing materialism and secularism. This is fertile ground for Freema-

---

48   W. Kirk MacNulty, *The Way of the Craftsman: Deluxe Edition* (Washington, D.C.: Plumbstone, 2017), 54.

sonry to cultivate a space for men to explore the mysteries of existence and the deeper currents of spiritual thought. Yet, the rituals and symbols of the Lodge, which were once gateways to profound contemplation, are often treated as formalities to be memorized and recited, rather than portals to deeper understanding.

Restoring the Speculative

The solution, then, might lie in a rebalance—recognizing that while the Lodge must necessarily handle certain administrative tasks, its true purpose is to engage men in the Royal Art of self-improvement, philosophical inquiry, and the search for transcendent truths.

The Lodge needs to be more than just a room where work gets done in the operational sense. It needs to be a place where Masons engage in the art of building themselves and others in a speculative sense. This requires a return to the philosophical roots of the craft—Hermeticism, Kabbalah, and the moral philosophies—that inspired figures like Robert Moray, John Theophilus Desaguliers, and even Preston himself. The symbols and rituals of Masonry are tools not just for governance but for transformation—both individual and collective.

The challenge for twenty-first-century Masonry is to restore the balance between Operative and speculative practices. This means shifting some of the energy that currently goes into logistics and operations back toward deeper engagement with the philosophical and spiritual dimensions of the craft. Lodges might consider:

- Reinvigorating the study of Masonic symbolism: Symbols like the square, compass, and trowel, right angles, and perpendiculars are not just elements of floorwork—they are metaphors for self-mastery, moral balance, and the construction of the soul. By returning to these symbols as gateways to wisdom, the speculative aspect can be restored.

- Creating space for philosophical discussion: Beyond the ritual, there should be time for Masons to engage with the speculative questions that animated the early brethren—questions about the nature of the divine, the mysteries of the universe, and the moral duties of man.
- Exploring the esoteric traditions: The roots of Freemasonry lie in deeper currents of esoteric thought—Kabbalistic, Hermetic, and alchemical traditions. These streams of wisdom should not be forgotten but explored as part of the Lodge's speculative work.
- Balancing service with reflection: While charity and service are important, they should not become the sole focus of the Lodge's activities. A thriving Lodge is one that balances its operational duties with moments of contemplation and inner work.

I propose that modern Freemasonry's focus has shifted too heavily toward the Operative side, with the day-to-day tasks of running a Lodge crowding out the more profound speculative practices that once defined the Craft. The way forward might lie in rediscovering the speculative dimension and rebalancing the Lodge's activities to cultivate both the external and internal aspects of Masonry in equal measure.

4

Applying the Beehive as a Model for Change

J ONATHAN SWIFT stands as a complex figure in the landscape of Freemasonry, using his sharp wit and satirical prowess to comment on the political and social issues of his time. While the extent of his direct involvement in Freemasonry remains debated, his profound understanding of its symbolism, history, and internal divisions—especially those related to the Jacobite-Hanoverian conflict—is evident in his work.

Swift's engagement with Freemasonry likely began around 1688 during his time at Trinity College, Dublin, where he contributed to a satirical play that alluded to the fraternity's practices and its Scottish origins.[49] This early contact, combined with his later ex-

49 Marsha Keith Schuchard, "Swift, Ramsay, and 'the Cabala, as Masonry Was Call'd in Those Days,'" *English Language Notes* 56, no. 1 (2018): 98.

periences in Ulster, where he encountered "Ancient" Scots-Irish Masonic traditions, provided him with ample inspiration for his satirical writings. His early interactions with Freemasonry set the stage for his later, more nuanced commentaries on the Craft.

Swift maintained close relationships with prominent Jacobite figures who were also Freemasons, including the Duke of Ormonde, Charles Boyle, and the Chevalier Andrew Michael Ramsay.[50] These associations influenced his perspective on Freemasonry, leading him to favor the Ancient Scots-Irish traditions over the Modern Hanoverian Grand Lodge, which he frequently ridiculed. Swift's alignment with Jacobite Freemasonry underscores his preference for traditions he viewed as more authentic and less politically compromised.

Knowledge of Esoteric Themes

Swift's writings reveal a deep familiarity with esoteric themes often associated with Freemasonry, including Kabalistic philosophy, Rosicrucianism, and even the symbolism of the beehive. He skillfully incorporated elements of Hebrew linguistics and numerology into his works, using these themes not only as tools for satire but also for political commentary.[51] Jonathan Swift was clearly adept in his ability to engage with complex Masonic ideas while maintaining his characteristic satirical tone.

Despite the satirical nature of his works, Swift's use of "drolling"—a form of humorous mockery—allowed him to explore sensitive political and religious topics while evading censorship.[52] This approach suggests that Swift's relationship with Freemasonry was more nuanced than mere mockery. His writings provide valuable

50   Schuchard, "Swift, Ramsay," 109.
51   Schuchard, "Swift, Ramsay," 106.
52   Schuchard, "Swift, Ramsay," 97

insights into the historical and philosophical foundations of the Craft, indicating a level of respect and understanding that transcends simple satire.

In his satirical essay, "A Letter from the Grand Mistress," Swift forges a fantastical history of Freemasonry, connecting it with ancient mythological figures, biblical references, and historical anecdotes, such as Fergus of Scotland being a Mason, the use of bees as Masonic symbols, and even references to "Druids" and "Cabalists."[53] Swift is skilled at creating elaborate, interconnected absurdities that sound scholarly but are complete nonsense.

Swift's use of the term "swarming" to describe the formation of new lodges parallels the political divisions of his time, particularly the rise of Jacobite lodges in opposition to the Hanoverian Grand Lodge.[54] This imagery suggests that Swift's use of bee symbolism extends beyond mere commentary on Masonic practices, touching upon broader social and political themes that were relevant to his contemporaries.

In short, Swift was not mocking Masonry from the outside, but engaging in a sophisticated form of insider satire that protected while it revealed, criticized while it preserved, and entertained while it informed.

53 Jonathan Swift, *The Works of Dr Jonathan Swift, Dean of St Patrick's, Dublin. Accurately Corrected by the Best Editions. With the Author's Life and Character; Notes Historical, Critical, and Explanatory; Tables of Contents, and Indexes. More Complete than Any Preceding Edition* (Edinburgh: printed for A. Donaldson, at Pope's Head, 1761), 8:329.

54 Schuchard, "Swift, Ramsay," 110.

Restoring Symbolism

What Swift said satirically in the eighteenth century, Walter Leslie Wilmshurst made practical in the twentieth century. In *The Way to the East*, he refers to the Supreme Grand Lodge as "a high and holy land… where the bees of Wisdom hive."[55] Wilmshurst's philosophical understanding is that a Mason may 'hive' with whom he wishes, but the holiest places are filled with gnosis and with those who work for the benefit of gnosis. His views, especially regarding spiritual enlightenment, underscore the importance of Lodges focusing on both ritual work and the deeper, esoteric side of Masonry. Wilmshurst implores us to reinforce the idea that Lodges must foster both intellectual and spiritual development.

In some ways, we are still recovering from the shift in the Masonic symbolism of the beehive, from the more profound meanings associated with the Third Degree to a simplified representation of industry.[56] This multifaceted symbol within Freemasonry, has often been simplified in its interpretation. Yet, contemporary Freemasons could fully appreciate and restore its deeper meanings. To this end, we must confirm the beehive as a central Masonic emblem, reminding Masons that the Lodge's success depends on both practical operations and intellectual engagement.

Practical Applications

Throughout various cultures and time periods, the bee has been associated with themes of death, the soul, and resurrection. These associations align closely with the Hiramic Legend, a central narrative of the Third Degree. Emphasizing the bee's symbolic link to

---

55 Walter Leslie Wilmshurst, *The Way to the East* (London: Watkins, 1938), 18.

56 Bullamore, "The Beehive and Freemasonry," 231.

mortality and the promise of resurrection could enrich the teachings of the Third Degree, providing a more profound understanding of the beehive's place within Masonic philosophy.

The beehive's intricate structure, organized society, and focus on the collective good make it an apt metaphor for a well-functioning Lodge. By highlighting this analogy, particularly in the context of the Third Degree, Freemasons can draw parallels between the beehive and an ideal Lodge culture—one where each member contributes to the greater good, ensuring the strength and harmony of the whole. This perspective reinforces the importance of unity, cooperation, and shared purpose within the Lodge.

While the beehive has long been associated with the virtue of industry, its symbolic depth extends far beyond this single attribute. For example, the beehive represents profound concepts, such as the immortality of the Order and the eternal nature of the Craft. Broadening the interpretation of the beehive allows Masons to better appreciate its role in conveying the enduring values of Freemasonry.

Future Directions

The beehive has served as a powerful stand-in for both Masonic Lodges and individual members. The beehive represented the ideal Lodge culture, where members worked together in harmony, much like bees, to build and sustain their community. The emphasis was on industry, diligence, and the collective pursuit of wisdom.

Masonic song celebrates the industriousness and excellence of the "flowers of the swarm"—those Masons who worked the hardest and produced the most valuable contributions. Honey represents the sweetness of intellectual and spiritual growth. Its production is the grand aim.

Take to heart the dire warning against intellectual laziness where idle Masons are compared to drones in a hive who didn't contribute and were eventually expelled. A Mason actively engages in the intellectual and spiritual life of the Lodge.

There is a clear need for modern Lodges to rebalance their focus, moving away from purely operational tasks and rediscovering the deeper, speculative work that Freemasonry was originally meant to explore. By doing so, the beehive could continue to serve as a symbol of both practical work and the pursuit of higher wisdom, guiding Masons in their personal collective growth.

PART
III

The
Speculative Hive

5

Honey as Wisdom

THE BEEHIVE IN FREEMASONRY is more than just a symbol of industry and cooperation; it holds a deeper, speculative meaning tied to the pursuit of wisdom. Honey, the product of the hive, symbolizes the sweet results of intellectual and spiritual inquiry within the Lodge.

Vedic Wisdom

Honey has traditionally been viewed as a symbol of knowledge and spiritual nourishment in various cultures and esoteric traditions. For example, in the Vedas, honey is described as a divine substance, symbolizing immortality and wisdom. In the *Rigveda*, composed between 1500 and 1000 BCE, honey is metaphorically associated with the fulfillment of desires and the acquisition of wisdom.

Honey in the Vedic tradition symbolizes sweetness, nourishment, and satisfaction. It becomes a metaphor for the desired outcome of the rituals—wisdom, prosperity, and the grace of the gods.[57] The *Rigveda* often refers to honey as a ceremonial offering,[58] but more frequently in an abstract and symbolic sense. The mention of honey as a source of wisdom is entangled with sacred rituals, the divine inspiration, and the attainment of wisdom.[59]

It is clear that within the *Rigveda*, honey is more than just a physical substance; it is a powerful symbol of the sweetness and richness that comes from divine favor, wisdom, and the fulfillment of spiritual and material desires. Somewhat later in the Vedic tradition comes the concept of *Madhu-vidyā* ("honey wisdom"), discussed in the Upanishads, composed between the eighth and fourth centuries BCE.[60] *Madhu-vidyā* emphasizes the mutual interdependence of all things, illustrating this through the analogy of honey and bees. It is often conceived as transmitted through initiation and in stages.[61]

Neoplatonic Understanding

The Neoplatonic philosopher Porphyry of Tyre (c. 234 – 305 CE) viewed honey as a symbol of multiple powers, possessing both ca-

57 *Rigveda* 1.90.6–8. Translation by Stephanie W. Jamison *&* Joel P. Brereton, eds., *The Rigveda: The Earliest Religious Poetry of India* (Oxford: Oxford University Press, 2014).

58 *Rigveda* 10.14.15, 10.154.1.

59 Honey is most often identified poetically with the drink *sóma* that produces ecstasy and enlightenment; see Rigveda 1.116.12, 1.154.4, 4.27.5, 4.58.1, 10–11, 7.101.1, 4, 8.48.1, 9.74.3 ("A great delight is the well-prepared somian honey...."), 10.94.3–4, 9, 10.123.3.

60 *Brihad-āranyaka* 2.5.1–19, *Chāndogya* 3.1–5. See R.C. Zaehner, *Hindu Scriptures* (New York: Everyman's Library, 1966), 58–61.

61 Aviva Robibo, *The Guru Tradition: India's Spiritual Heritage* (New York: Lexington Books, 2024).

thartic and preservative qualities. In *On the Cave of the Nymphs in the Thirteenth Book of the Odyssey*, Porphyry interprets the cave described in Homer's *Odyssey* as a symbol laden with various esoteric meanings.

In this context, bees and honey are symbolic elements associated with the Naiades, the nymphs presiding over waters. Specifically, it is mentioned that bees deposit their honey in amphorae and bowls within the cave.[62] Honey in this symbolism represents nourishment and preservation; it is linked to the sustenance provided by the bees, which are considered sacred or divine in certain traditions.

Porphyry also connects honey to the purification rituals in mystery cults, particularly the Leontic rites, where honey is used for purification instead of water. This association is extended to the realm of divine or mystical experiences, where honey is seen as a substance that preserves from decay and symbolizes the pleasure that binds souls to the process of generation or material existence.[63]

Furthermore, the text refers to the bees themselves as symbols of souls, particularly those who live justly and return to their divine origins after their earthly lives. This connection is further enriched by references to mythological tales where honey plays a role in divine intoxication and binding, illustrating the influence of pleasure and generation on divine beings.[64]

For Porphyry, honey and bees are rich in symbolic meaning, relating to nourishment, purity, preservation, and the cyclical nature of life and death, particularly in relation to the soul's journey through the material world and back to the divine.

62   Porphyry, *On the Cave of the Nymphs in the Thirteenth Book of the Odyssey*, trans. Thomas Taylor (London: J.M. Watkins, 1917), 7.

63   Porphyry, *On the Cave of the Nymphs*, 20.

64   Porphyry, *On the Cave of the Nymphs*, 21.

Honey as Masonic Charity

In 1741, Fifield D'Assigny penned a vigorous defense of Freemason-ry after the brethren came under criticism. An engraving included in this work depicted an allegorical figure of Masonic Charity, that:

> Represented [Charity] in the form of a naked Babe, having a sprightly Countenance, and surrounded with a Cloud; in its Right Hand holding a bloody Heart, in its Left, affording Honey to a Bee without Wings; which Draught seems to Import, that Charity ought to be as humble as a Child, and all her Gifts bestowed with a chearful Will. The bleeding Heart must signify, the pain a good Brother feels when he sees, and pitys the Distressed: And that Honey which is given to the Bee without Wings, is that Succour which should be afforded to the Unfortunate who cannot help Themselves.[65]

As individual Masons could be thought of as bees, the symbolism here is very apt. The Freemason who has fallen into misfortune re-sembles a bee that has lost its wings. D'Assigny's imaginative image offers relief to in the symbolic form of honey.

Sacred Beauty

There is a common Masonic prayer that asks for divine wisdom so that a candidate might be taught to embody what the book

---

65   Fifield D'Assigny, *An Impartial Answer to the Enemies of Free-Masonry, wherein Their unjust Suspicions, and idle Reproaches of that Honourable Craft, are briefly Rehearsed, and clearly Confuted* (Dublin: Printed by Edward Waters in Dames' street and are to be sold at his Shop, and at Mr. Richard Pinder's at the White Hart in Pembroke Court, [1741]), 15–16.

of Psalms calls the הדרי־קדש or the "beauties of holiness."[66] This phrase has undergone many transformations! The changes are masterfully tracked in Robert Davis's *The Mason's Words*. The first known printing of the prayer is the 1730 printing of John Pennell's Irish *Constitutions*.

> And we beseech thee, O LORD God, to bless this our present undertaking, and grant that this, our new Brother, may dedicate his life to thy Service, and be a true and faithful Brother among us, endue him with Divine Wisdom, that he may, with the Secrets of Masonry, be able to unfold the Mysteries of Godliness and Christianity. This we humbly beg in the Name and for the sake of Jesus Christ our Lord and Savior.[67]

This prayer must have been well known in the early grand lodge era because William Preston included a version in his 1772 *Illustrations*.

> Vouchsafe thy aid, Almighty Father and supreme governor of the world, on this our present convention; and grant that this candidate for masonry may dedicate and devote his life to thy service, and become a true and faithful brother among us. Endue him with a competence of thy divine wisdom, that, by the secrets of this art, he may be better enabled to unfold the mysteries of godliness, to the honor of thy holy name. Amen.[68]

Preston would change the prose in later editions. Towards the end of his life, the prayer had changed slightly:

66 Psalm 110:3; cf. 96:9.

67 Robert G. Davis, *The Mason's Words: The History and Evolution of the American Masonic Ritual* (Guthrie, Okla.: Building Stone Publishing, 2013), 71.

68 Preston, *Illustrations of Masonry: A Grand Gala in Honour of Free Masonry, Held at the Crown and Anchor Tavern, in the Strand,* 209–10.

Vouchsafe thine aid, Almighty Father of the Universe, to this our present convention and grant that this Candidate for Masonry may dedicate and devote his life to thy service, and become a true and faithful Brother among us! Endue him with a competency of thy divine wisdom; that, by the secrets of this Art, he may be the better enabled to display the beauties of godliness, to the honour of thy holy Name! Amen.[69]

It would be changed again by Jeremy Cross to become the "beauties of holiness."[70] This transformation is interesting, but it's a verb that should catch our attention: The ability to "unfold" became the ability to "display," because these two words are more alike than conventional usage would indicate.

Our word "display" derives from Old French ("*despletier*" or "*desplier*") and Latin ("*displicare*"), meaning "to scatter, disperse, or unfold." These roots suggest a process of gradual revelation, much like a flower unfurling its petals to expose its inner beauty. This action of unfolding—whether it's a banner, a sail, or an abstract concept like virtue—is central to the word's meaning. The connection between "display" and natural processes like flowering emphasizes the organic, almost inevitable nature of revealing what is hidden, a process deeply embedded in Masonic rituals where truths are gradually uncovered and made visible to the initiate; where hidden qualities are brought into the light, much like a flower's inner beauty becomes visible as it blooms.

The metaphor of a flower opening not only illustrates the revelation of beauty but also highlights its role in sustaining life. As a flower blooms, it provides nectar, which bees collect and transform

69 William Preston, *Illustrations of Masonry*, 12th ed. (London: Printed for G. Wilkie, No 57, Paternoster-Row., 1812), 35.

70 Jeremy Ladd Cross, *The True Masonic Chart, or Hieroglyphic Monitor; Containing All the Emblems Explained in the Degrees....* (New Haven, Conn.: T. Woodward, 1826), 14.

into honey. This natural process parallels the Masonic prayer's request for divine wisdom, suggesting that wisdom, like nectar, is a gift from the divine, which through effort and collective action, becomes something valuable and nourishing—like honey.

In this context, the act of "displaying the beauties of Godliness" is akin to a flower revealing its nectar, offering the potential for creating something greater. Just as the quality of honey depends on the purity of the nectar, the wisdom and virtues cultivated in Masonry are most potent when they originate from a sincere and divine source. The prayer embodies this idea, asking not only for the individual revelation of virtues but for these virtues to contribute to the collective good, much like bees working together to produce honey. It is the flowering of wisdom within a Mason, which then attracts other Masons—like bees—to gather this nectar of knowledge. As bees create honey from this nectar, so too do Masons create collective wisdom from the insights of individual brothers. This creates a spiral of cause and effect, where the wisdom of one Mason enriches the Lodge, inspiring others to seek and produce more wisdom, perpetuating the cycle.

Biblical Wisdom

In Masonic tradition, the bee and the beehive are powerful symbols that represent a range of virtues, including industry, foresight, and collective effort. These symbols are deeply intertwined with scriptural teachings, where they are often associated with themes of labor, prosperity, and spiritual growth. However, as Charles C. Hunt illustrates in *A Masonic Concordance of the Holy Bible*, these symbols also carry profound metaphysical meanings that connect to traditional doctrines of resurrection, eternal life, and the soul's journey.

Wisdom and Labor

Proverbs advises us to observe the ant's industriousness as a model for human behavior.[71] In Masonic symbolism, the ant, like the bee, exemplifies the virtues of hard work and foresight.[72] Both creatures diligently prepare for the future, a principle that Masons are encouraged to embody in their own lives. This self-motivated labor is akin to the bee's contribution to the hive, where each individual's effort benefits the entire community.

Ephesians and Titus reinforce the importance of honest, productive labor, a key Masonic value.[73] In Masonic tradition, the beehive represents not only individual effort but also the collective benefit of such labor. Each bee works not just for its own survival but for the well-being of the entire hive, mirroring the Masonic ideal of contributing to society through diligent and virtuous work.

The book of Proverbs consistently highlights themes of diligence, foresight, and the rewards of hard work. These teachings align perfectly with Masonic values, where the industrious Mason, symbolized by the bee, is celebrated for his consistent and thoughtful work that benefits both himself and the community.

Divine Promise and Abundance

In Exodus, the promise of a "land flowing with milk and honey" symbolizes not just physical abundance but the fruits of labor in a well-ordered society.[74] Similarly, Psalms emphasizes that even in the most unlikely places, God provides sustenance, symbolized

71   Proverbs 6:6–8.
72   Charles C. Hunt, *Masonic Concordance of the Holy Bible* (Bloomington, Ill.: Masonic Book Club, 1984), 47.
73   Ephesians 4:28, Titus 3:14.
74   Exodus 3:8.

by honey from the rock.[75] For Masons, these verses highlight the rewards of diligent work in hope of divine blessings, reinforcing the idea that labor guided by higher principles leads to prosperity and fulfillment.

Honey's role as a valuable commodity reflects its connection to wealth and commerce.[76] In Masonry, this aspect of honey reinforces the idea that industry and labor produce valuable outcomes, both materially and spiritually. The trade of honey symbolizes the fruits of diligent work, which benefit the individual and the community, mirroring the Masonic principle of mutual dependence and the collective effort symbolized by the beehive.

Resurrection and Immortality

Samson's encounter with bees and honey in the lion's carcass presents a powerful metaphor for resurrection and new life.[77] While the biblical riddle illustrates the emergence of life from death, Charles C. Hunt interprets the lion as a representation of death, the bees as the immortal soul, and the honey as the sweetness of eternal life.[78] This aligns with the Masonic belief in the immortality of the soul and the transformative power of divine wisdom, where the bee and honey symbolize not only industry but also the soul's journey through death to life eternal.

Paul's teaching on resurrection in Corinthians also ties to a Masonic interpretation of the bee as a symbol of eternal life.[79] Hunt connects this epistle to Samson's riddle, where the sweetness of honey emerging from the carcass of the lion symbolizes life trium-

75   Psalms 81:16.

76   Genesis 43:11, Ezekiel 27:17.

77   Judges 14:8.

78   Hunt, *Masonic Concordance*, 48.

79   1 Corinthians 15:53–55.

phing over death. This reinforces the Masonic belief in the soul's immortality and the ultimate victory of life over death, with the bee and honey serving as enduring symbols of this profound truth.

Collective Action

Scripture also uses bees metaphorically to describe enemies that are swift, organized, and overwhelming.[80] This comparison illustrates the power of collective action, a theme central to Masonic teachings. The bee and the beehive symbolize the strength that comes from unity and cooperation, where each Mason, like a bee, contributes to the collective good, ensuring the prosperity of the whole.

The beehive, as a Masonic symbol, encapsulates a broad spectrum of virtues—industry, foresight, collective effort, and the transformative power of labor. Yet, as Hunt emphasizes, it also symbolizes deeper spiritual truths, such as resurrection, eternal life, and the immortality of the soul. By engaging in diligent labor, Masons not only contribute to material and societal wealth but also participate in the divine process of spiritual growth and resurrection. The beehive thus represents both the practical and the metaphysical, guiding Masons in their pursuit of personal and collective enlightenment, and ensuring the prosperity of future generations.

Practical Implementation

By drawing on the rich symbolism and lessons associated with the beehive, Lodges can create programs and practices that foster intellectual and spiritual growth, helping members move beyond the ritual to cultivate true Masonic wisdom.

80   Psalms 118:10–12, Deuteronomy 1:44.

LODGE PROGRAMS

The beehive teaches us the value of collective knowledge and the importance of each member contributing to the whole. By creating intellectual programs, Lodges can emulate the beehive's structure, encouraging members to share their insights and wisdom. Here are some ways contemporary Freemasons could imitate the practice:

STUDY CIRCLES AND DISCUSSION GROUPS. Encourage your members to form study circles or discussion groups that focus on Masonic philosophy, symbolism, and esoteric traditions. These groups can operate much like a beehive, with each member contributing their knowledge to create a richer understanding for all. Regular meetings can be organized where specific texts or topics are discussed, promoting continuous learning and engagement. For example, a Lodge could establish a monthly study group focused on the works of James Anderson, Laurence Dermott, William Preston, Thaddeus Mason Harris, and so many other outstanding contributors to our understanding of the *Royal Art*. For lodges or individual Masons seeking additional support or alternative formats, the Masonic Formation Academy offers an online forum where such discussions can take place, ensuring these opportunities are available to all.

LECTURE SERIES AND GUEST SPEAKERS. Propose organizing a lecture series that features knowledgeable Masons or external experts on topics related to the speculative aspects of Freemasonry. These lectures can serve as "honey," nourishing the intellectual life of the Lodge. By inviting speakers with expertise in areas such as Hermeticism, Kabbalah, or the history of Freemasonry, Lodges can provide members with new perspectives and deeper insights. For example, host a quarterly lecture where scholars present on the influence of Hermeticism on Renaissance thought and its connection to Masonic philosophy, or perhaps discussions of how contemporary academies differ from classical *trivium* and *quadrivium*.

RITUAL UNDERSTANDING. Suggest ways to integrate periods of reflection and meditation into Masonic rituals. By allowing time for members to contemplate the deeper meanings of the symbols and lessons they encounter, Lodges can help Masons transform ritual into a more personal and enlightening experience. An example of this is introducing a moment of silence or guided meditation after the opening of a Lodge meeting, where members can reflect on the symbolism of the working tools, or to remember brethren who have gone to the Celestial Lodge. This can be even more powerful if you can light a candle.

ESOTERIC STUDIES. Encourage Lodges to explore esoteric traditions that align with Masonic principles, such as Kabbalah, Hermeticism, or biblical scholarship. By studying these traditions, Masons can deepen their understanding of the Craft and the universal truths it embodies. Lodges could organize study groups or workshops focused on these esoteric traditions, helping members explore their connections to Freemasonry. A Lodge might offer a series of workshops on the Tree of Life in Kabbalah, exploring its symbolism and potential relevance to Masonic teachings.

Personal Growth through Continuous Learning

To ensure the ongoing intellectual and spiritual development of its members, a Lodge must embody a mindset focused on continuous learning. Such a mindset values the process and the learning experience, regardless of the result.[81] The beehive's model of collective

81   Carol S. Dweck, *Mindset: The New Psychology of Success* (New York: Ballantine Books, 2007), 48.

effort and mutual support can be applied to create a dynamic learning environment within the Lodge.

Advocate for the establishment of mentorship programs where more experienced Masons guide newer members in their intellectual and spiritual development, as we might imagine older bees teaching the younger ones the art of making honey. This mentorship can help new members integrate more fully into the Lodge and deepen their understanding of Masonic principles. To do this, you could pair each new initiate with a seasoned mentor who guides them through the study of key Masonic texts and symbols during their first year in the Lodge.

Propose interactive workshops where members can engage in hands-on activities that explore Masonic symbols, rituals, and philosophies in depth. These workshops can provide a more dynamic and engaging learning experience, allowing members to actively participate in their education rather than passively receiving information. Host a workshop where members create their own Masonic toasts, songs, poems, and other creative endeavors for the benefit of the Lodge.

Personal Growth through Continuous Learning

In the ever-changing landscape of the modern world, a Masonic Lodge must continuously strive to maintain its relevance and vitality. The beehive, a sometimes overlooked symbol in Freemasonry, represents not only industry and collective effort but also adaptability and resilience—qualities that are crucial for the ongoing growth and prosperity of a Lodge. Lodges can honor their rich traditions while embracing innovative approaches to education, community engagement, and intellectual development.

A Lodge's ability to thrive depends on its capacity to balance the preservation of time-honored Masonic practices with the adoption of new, innovative ideas—even when those new ideas may actually be rooted in older traditions. This balance ensures that the Lodge remains both a stable institution and a dynamic force capable of attracting and retaining members in the twenty-first century.

Traditional Masonic practices—rituals, lectures, orations, mythopoeia, and the symbols passed down through generations—form the bedrock of the Craft. These elements connect Masons to their historical roots and provide a sense of continuity and identity. Preserving and respecting these traditions is crucial, as they offer members a deep sense of belonging and a tangible link to the ancient wisdom of the fraternity. Lodges should hold regular ritual rehearsals and historical lectures to ensure that the traditional aspects of Freemasonry are well-understood and appreciated by all members. This not only reinforces the continuity of Masonic teachings but also strengthens the collective identity of the Lodge.

It is not in the power of any man, or Body of men, to make any alteration, or innovation in the body of Masonry without the consent first obtained of the annual Grand Lodge. Care must be taken within a Masonic Lodge that change does not mean abandoning tradition, but rather enhancing it. By integrating modern technology and educational tools, Lodges can make traditional practices more accessible and engaging for members. For instance, the introduction of online study resources and digital archives can complement in-person Lodge activities, making it easier for members to participate and learn, regardless of geographical constraints. It is easier than ever to create an online platform where members have access to Masonic texts, virtual discussion forums, and live-streamed lectures. As a supplement only, this platform would not only preserve traditional teachings but also adapt them to meet the needs of contemporary members who may be unable to attend every in-person gathering.

Community Engagement

The beehive's symbolism of collective effort extends beyond the Lodge itself, underscoring the importance of contributing to the broader community. Freemasonry, with its focus on moral and ethical teachings, has much to offer the world. By extending intellectual programs and Masonic wisdom to the public, Lodges can build stronger connections with their communities, enhancing both the visibility and understanding of Freemasonry.

Community outreach provides an opportunity for Lodges to share the "honey" of Masonic wisdom with those outside the fraternity. Through public lectures, workshops, and discussions on the principles of Freemasonry, Lodges can demystify the Craft and highlight its relevance to contemporary ethical and philosophical issues. This type of engagement can also help dispel misconceptions about Freemasonry, fostering a more positive public perception. Organize a series of public lectures covering topics such as the historical contributions of Freemasons to society, the ethical teachings of the Craft, or the Liberal Arts and Sciences. These events could be open to both Masons and non-Masons, creating an opportunity for broader community involvement and understanding.

By actively engaging with the community, Lodges can play a pivotal role in educating the public about the values and principles of Freemasonry. This engagement not only strengthens the Lodge's ties with the community but also attracts potential new members who resonate with the Masonic ideals of brotherhood, charity, and truth. Many Lodges partner with local school districts. Offer educational workshops or seminars at local schools, universities, or community centers, focusing on the philosophical and ethical foundations of Freemasonry. These programs can serve as an introduction to Masonic thought for those interested in exploring the Craft further, potentially leading to new membership.

Planning for Lodge Growth

To ensure a Lodge's growth and prosperity, balancing tradition with adaptation and engaging with the community are essential strategies. By living the lessons of the beehive—industry, cooperation, and adaptability—Lodges can remain vibrant and relevant in an ever-changing world. These practices not only preserve the rich heritage of Freemasonry but also ensure that it continues to flourish as a force for intellectual and spiritual growth in the modern era. Masonic Lodges need only apply speculative principles to ensure their ongoing growth and vitality. By embracing both tradition and technology, and by reaching out to the community, Lodges can build a dynamic and forward-thinking environment that honors the past while preparing for the future.

Honey, as a product of the beehive, represents the sweet results of intellectual and spiritual inquiry, symbolizing the wisdom that emerges from diligent study and reflection. By examining the role of honey in different cultural and philosophical contexts, we see how this symbol has been used to convey deeper meanings related to knowledge, preservation, and the soul's journey.

The beehive—as industry and cooperation—also teaches us the value of collective effort in the pursuit of enlightenment. In Masonic practice, this translates to the importance of working together to cultivate wisdom, both individually and as a community. Masons are called to engage in continuous learning and intellectual exploration, ensuring that the wisdom they seek is both profound and enduring.

True knowledge is both a personal journey and a shared endeavor. The beehive serves as a powerful metaphor for the way in which Masons can work together to build a rich storehouse of wisdom, from which all can draw nourishment.

6

Masonic Education and Intellectual Engagement

ASONIC EDUCATION has historically been a cornerstone of the Craft, but in many Lodges today, its role
has diminished. I once heard a Past Master say that we
owe William Preston for, "Making this a thinking man's game." Such
a statement is not only inaccurate, it is misleading and offensive.
We are indebted to William Preston for a great many things in this
fraternity, but the aspiration for knowledge has been a key feature
since the conception.

The Regius Poem, contained within a document called the Hal-
liwell Manuscript, offers compelling historical evidence that education, particularly through the lens of the liberal arts and sciences,
has been integral to the Masonic tradition from its earliest days.

This manuscript (c. 1425) frames the craft of Masonry not merely as a manual labor or technical skill, but as an intellectual pursuit deeply connected to the study of geometry, moral philosophy, and broader educational ideals.

> *Vro3gh hýe grace · of criſt ýn heven ·*
> *He commensed · ýn þe fýens ſeven ·* [82]

> Through the high grace of Christ in heaven
> He [Euclid] commenced in the sciences seven

The poem explicitly attributes the origins of the Craft to Euclid, the famed Greek mathematician, positioning the study of geometry as foundational to the moral and ethical teachings of early Masons. Furthermore, the document underscores the importance of knowledge and learning, suggesting that Masons were expected to cultivate not just technical proficiency but also intellectual and moral refinement.

By advocating for the study of the seven liberal arts and sciences—particularly geometry, which it treats as the highest of these disciplines—the Regius Poem affirms that education was embedded in the Masonic tradition from its inception. This manuscript stands as historical proof that the pursuit of wisdom, both practical and philosophical, was a core value of the Craft long before the formalization of speculative Freemasonry in the eighteenth century.

With the liberal education recommended to each member of the Lodge, the knowledge of the Masons took on an otherworldly quality. For example, *The Muses Threnodie* (1638) by Henry Adamson is a lengthy, multi-faceted poem that combines elements of elegy, topographical description, and historical reflection. Adamson continues the mysterious applications of knowledge stating:

---

82 British Library Royal MS 17 A.i, lines 555–56.

Thus Gall assured me it would be so,
And my good genius truly doth it know:
For what we do presage is not in grosse,
For we be brethren of the rosie cross;
We have the mason-word and second sight,
Things for to come we can foretell aright....[83]

Non-Masons at that time were also aware of the Mysterious nature of Masonic lexicons. Robert Kirk in the 1691 printing of *The Secret Commonwealth of Elves, Fauns and Fairies* shared what he knew of the Masons Word and Second Sight as two of the "five curiosities" he found in Scotland. Kirk describes:

> The Mason Word, which tho some make a Misterie of it, I will not conceal a little of what I know. It is lyke a Rabbinical Tradition, in way of Comment on Jachin and Boaz, the two Pillars erected in Solomon's Temple, (1 Kings, 7. 21.) with ane Addition of some secret Signe delyvered from Hand to Hand, by which they know and become familiar one with another.[84]

> This Second Sight, so largely treated of before.[85]

Such statements from the pre-Grand Lodge British Isles represent fields of hidden knowledge. Consider how an artisan with information about Astrology, Geometry, and the like might train another

83 Henry Adamson, *The Muses Threnodie, or, Mirthfull Mournings, on the Death of Master Gall Containing Varietie of Pleasant Poëticall Descriptions, Morall Instructions, Historiall Narrations, and Divine Observations, with the Most Remarkable Antiquities of Scotland, Especially at Perth* (Printed at Edinburgh: In King Iames College, by George Anderson, 1638), 32.

84 Robert Kirk, *The Secret Commonwealth of Elves, Fauns, and Fairies* (Aberfoyle, 1691), 64.

85 Kirk, 64–65.

who did not. The ability to plan ahead and carry out long-term projects by interpreting the Book of Nature would absolutely seem like magic and have been akin to something like 'Second Sight' to the uninitiated. The often quoted Third Law from Arthur C. Clarke states, "Any sufficiently advanced technology is indistinguishable from magic."[86] Masons are, and always have been, crafty users of magical technologies.

Modern Challenges

Another significant challenge to Masonic education, both historically and today, is the presence of what early Freemasons referred to as False Brethren. These were men who joined the fraternity not for the pursuit of knowledge or the Craft's higher ideals, but for personal gain, curiosity, or social advantages. As Christopher B. Murphy points out, False Brethren posed a real threat to the integrity of the Lodge, as they did not grasp or respect the deeper intellectual and spiritual values that define Freemasonry.[87] The admission of such individuals diluted the purpose of the Lodge, reducing it in some cases to a mere social club—an idea that is at the heart of what has been coined the "Tavern Myth."[88]

This myth wrongly assumes that early Masonic lodges were primarily social clubs focused on indulgence and camaraderie rather

86   Arthur C. Clarke, "Clarke's Third Law on UFO's," *Science* 159, no. 3812 (January 19, 1968): 255.

87   Christopher B. Murphy, "Assessing Authentic Lodge Culture: Moving Beyond the Tavern Myth," in *Exploring Early Grand Lodge Freemasonry: Studies in Honor of the Tricentennial of the Establishment of the Grand Lodge of England*, ed. Christopher B. Murphy and Shawn Eyer (Washington, D.C.: Plumbstone, 2017), 409–15.

88   Christopher B. Murphy, "The Tavern Myth: Reassessing the Culture of Early Grand Lodge Era Freemasonry," *Philalethes: The Journal of Masonic Research and Letters* 68, no. 2 (2015): 51.

than intellectual or spiritual work. While early lodges did meet in taverns—then the civic centers of many towns—the setting did not define the substance of their meetings.[89] The rigorous expectations of decorum and temperance, outlined in documents such as the *Old Charges* and Anderson's *Constitutions*, demonstrate that Freemasonry was a serious intellectual and spiritual pursuit. According to Murphy, early Freemasons saw themselves as stewards of an ancient, divinely inspired institution, and it was this sense of higher purpose, not mere socialization, that attracted the most prominent and educated members of society.[90]

The implication by many that the guild Masons were unlearned, uninteresting, and unintelligent would render the fact that Gentlemen such as Robert Moray and others of the Royal Society were seeking to associate with them a truly puzzling occurrence. It seems that the contemporary telling of this story reads as though the intelligentsia of high society decided to infiltrate and commandeer the stone guilds in order to start a dinner club. This assumption, of course, tends to ignore that there were "speculative" Lodges constructing actual edifices as late as 1793, when Federal Lodge Nº 1 in the District of Columbia was working on the Capitol Building under the direction of their charter Master, James Hoban. This Lodge played a crucial role in society, hosting many important ceremonies and events.[91]

Since the distinctions between "Operative" and "Speculative" don't seem to indicate what many have long believed, why is there

---

89   Murphy, "Assessing Authentic Lodge Culture,"391.

90   Christopher B. Murphy, "Assessing Authentic Lodge Culture: Moving Beyond the Tavern Myth," in *Exploring Early Grand Lodge Freemasonry: Studies in Honor of the Tricentennial of the Establishment of the Grand Lodge of England*, ed. Christopher B. Murphy and Shawn Eyer (Washington, D.C.: Plumbstone, 2017), 392.

91   B. Christopher Ruli, *The White House and the Freemasons* (Richmond, Va.: Macoy, 2023), 18–21.

still a war on Masonic education? Maybe it's a question of seman-
tics. After all, the ancient mysteries were communicated in 'schools'
and the Rosicrucians operated the 'invisible college.' Teaching and
learning for the sake of posterity is at the heart of what we do as
Freemasons.

Just because our current challenges are, well, current, should not
imply in any way that they are new. For example, the persistence of
False Brethren in early Freemasonry prompted figures like Edward
Oakley, a Freemason and Architect, to chastise those "weak and
very unworthy" members who joined the Craft in a "vain flight of
curiosity" or for "Pride and Ambition," failing to understand the
true purpose of Masonic labor.[92]

Oakley was incensed by the lack of desire for learning. He took
the obligations his installation so seriously that, upon becoming
Master of his Lodge in 1728, he reminded the brethren:

> I am likewise in Duty bound to acquaint you, that it is highly
> necessary for the Improvement of the Members of a Lodge, that
> such Instruments and Books be provided, as be convenient and
> useful in the Exercise, and for the Advancement of this Divine
> Science of Masonry, and that proper Lectures be constantly read
> in such of the Sciences, as shall be thought to be most agreeable
> to the Society, and to the Honour and Instruction of the Craft.[93]

Oakley was strongly associated with the restoration of Classical
architecture in London and the move away from Gothic architecture.[94] In like manner, I call for us to restore Classical education to

---

92   Benjamin Cole, *The Antient Constitutions of the Free and Accepted*
     Masons, the Second Edition. (London: printed for B. Creake, at
     the Red Bible in Ave-Mary-Lane, Ludgate-Street, near St. Paul's;
     and B. Cole Engraver, the Corner of King's Head-Court, near
     Fetter-Lane, Holbourn, 1731), 31.

93   Cole, 30–31.

94   Shawn Eyer, "This Divine Science: Architecture and Speculative

the Masonic Lodge. The time has come to recognize that the secret to saving the Craft is individually admitting what we don't know and letting others take over in those spots. We all have a Swiss cheese education. Our brethren should help fill in the holes. This, of course, must start with the Master.

Repeated and well-sourced Masonic scholarship in the twenty-first century has completely destroyed the argument that early speculative Masonry was nothing but a group of drunken libertines. And yet, like the satirical Black Knight fighting King Arthur, some Masons continue to hop around one-legged. This battle is over. Masonry is, and always has been, a thinking man's game.

Future Directions

Humans are behaviorally adaptive creatures. Our evolution happens memetically more than physiologically. Gaps in knowledge can be deadly, so we have adapted to share the knowledge of experience for the continuance of the species. More generally speaking, this means that for the species to evolve efficiently, each individual's labors must also be in some way useful to the whole. Each has a duty; each exercises it for the good of all, and there is always work to be done. One of William Preston's "friendly admonitions"[95] is a poetic reframing of a message from Charles Leslie that the work is finally the point. Leslie's 1741 "Vindication of Masonry" states:

> Knowledge must be attained by degrees, nor is it every where to be found. Wisdom seeks the secret shade, the lonely cell designed for contemplation, there inthroned she sits, and there delivers her

Freemasonry," The George Washington Masonic National Memorial (blog), 2015.

95 William Preston, *Illustrations of Masonry*, 2nd ed. (London: Printed for J. Wilkie, No. 71. St. Paul's Church Yard, 1775), 25.

oracles; seek her, pursue the real bliss, tho' the passage be difficult, the further we trace it, the easier it will become.[96]

The path to Masonic light is not easy, nor was it ever supposed to be. In fact, Divine intervention is invoked while traveling the "rugged path of life."[97] We are suddenly revived, because the work of the Lodge is done together, with many hands to lift the burdens.

Structured Programs

The implementation of structured educational programs within Freemasonry has been a concern for the fraternity since its earliest days as a speculative institution. The 300th anniversary of modern Freemasonry has come and gone, and it is instructive to examine historical approaches to Masonic education and consider how they can inform our current practices.

In 1890, G.W. Speth, Secretary of Quatuor Coronati Lodge № 2076, published "A Masonic Curriculum" in response to the question "what books should a young English student read in order to master the rudiments of Masonic history?"[98] This comprehen-

96 Charles Leslie, "A Vindication of Masonry, and its Excellency Demonstrated in a Discourse at the Consecration of the Lodge Vernon Kilwinning, on May 15, 1741, by Charles Leslie, M.A. Master-Mason and Member of that Lodge." In *The Free Masons Pocket-companion* (Edinburgh: Printed by Auld, and Smellie, and sold at their Printing House, Morocco's Close, Lawn-Market, M,DCC,LXV [1765]), 162.

97 Thomas Smith Webb, *The Freemason's Monitor; or, Illustrations of Masonry: In Two Parts* (New York: Printed by Southwick and Crooker No. 354, Water-Street, 1802),, 143.

98 G.W. Speth, "A Masonic Curriculum," *Ars Quatuor Coronatorum, Being the Transactions of the Quatuor Coronati Lodge No. 2076* 3 (1890): 116.

sive guide to Masonic study provides valuable insights into late nineteenth-century approaches to Masonic education and offers a framework that remains relevant today.

Speth divided Masonic study into six interconnected sections:

1. History (legendary and authentic)
2. Symbolism and Ethics
3. Jurisprudence
4. Ritual
5. General Masonic knowledge
6. Specialized topics

He emphasizes that these areas are "often concurrent and interdependent," which highlights the holistic nature of Masonic education.[99]

Speth's curriculum provides a model for tiered learning that can be adapted for modern use. He recommends that the student's studies "must be gradual and progressive, and that he must not attempt too much at first."[100]

For new initiates:

- Begin with foundational knowledge of guild history and medieval architecture.
- Progress to studying the Old Charges and early Masonic documents.
- Introduce the history of Grand Lodges and the development of modern Freemasonry.

For experienced members:

- Masonic symbolism and ethics.
- Study Masonic jurisprudence and ritual development.
- Encourage specialization in areas of Masonic research.

99   Speth, "A Masonic Curriculum," 116.
100   Speth, 117.

We have already discussed how mentor programs pairing experienced Masons with new initiates have become increasingly popular in many Grand Lodges. Later, we'll explore how these programs align well with models of adult learning, particularly the principles of self-concept and the role of experience. Mentorship programs can support this self-concept by providing guidance while still allowing the mentee to take responsibility for their own learning.

Regular one-on-one meetings or class-based sessions between mentor and mentee, following a structured curriculum, can address multiple andragogical principles. The structured curriculum ensures that learning is oriented towards real-life application. By covering Masonic history, symbolism, and personal development, these sessions can demonstrate the immediate relevance of the learning to the Mason's life and Masonic journey.

Ask any Millennial Freemason and they will tell you about at least one conversation they have had with an older brother, usually of a particular generation, about what the older brother will call, "the esoterics." Within this conversation, the word will have been uttered with moderate-to-strong disgust and in hushed tones. It's as though these brothers believe that if they say the word too many times they will summon some very old occult evil.

It's easy to see where these brothers are wrong, but it is important to understand they are also *not* wrong. Many of these brothers have had to suffer through Lodge programs where everything from alchemy, Rosicrucianism, Theosophy, and even Chakra healing—all in the name of Masonry! I have experienced first hand presentations on pop culture topics such as whether Harry Potter was a Mason and the musical *CATS* as Masonic allegory. Suffice it to say, Beetlejuice might not come if you say "esoteric" too frequently, but that doesn't mean the result won't be something equally absurd.

This is because, while many of these topics are adjacent to Freemasonry, they are patently not Masonry. Many well-meaning Masons—who thought they had entered into a secret society—were disillusioned by Masonry at the dawn of the twenty-first century and these brothers sought to add elements of the contemplative environment and New Age spirituality as a means of filling the perceived void. This backfired horribly and left many Masons firmly drawing lines in the sand against Masonic education. The baby was lost in the water.

The mistake was to attempt to create new esoteric practices. If you want to display the beauty of what is hidden, you have to examine your own practice. The Mystic Tie that connects all brethren also leads to the pathway not yet traveled. This evokes the poetic wisdom given by Bashō to his disciple as he prepared for a journey in 1693. The words are *Kojin no ato wo motomezu, kojin no motometaru tokoro wo motomeyo*—Don't try for what the men of old left behind; try for what they were trying to achieve.[101] My feeling is that this is mostly accomplished through the acting of asking questions:

- What literature did they read?
- What scientific means did they have of understanding the cosmos?
- What knowledge were they desperate to perpetuate?
- What is hidden in plain sight?
- Are there etymological clues in the Hebrew words we use?
- Can you locate the four classical elements in the Craft degrees?
- How many references to we find to our Ancient brother, Pythagoras?

The supreme secret of fraternity is learning to love living in mystery. There is no shortage of rich spiritual lessons to be extracted from the work. After all, Freemasonry can be considered the greatest uninterrupted esoteric tradition in the world. Freemasons must celebrate it and protect it. Otherwise, Freemasons interested in these

---

101   William Ritchie Wilson, "The Truth of Haikai," *Monumenta Nipponica* 26, no. 1/2 (1971): 49.

topics will continue to be met with Crystal Healing Reiki practice at best, and a hazing tuxedo club at worst.

In recent years, there's been a noticeable shift away from organized religion, but this does not necessarily equate to an increase in atheism. Many people today still consider themselves spiritual or theistic, though they do not practice a formal religion. Freemasonry, with its broad spiritual framework, has long provided a space where men can pursue shared moral and spiritual principles without being confined by dogma. Masons have always been obligated only "to that Religion in which all Men agree."[102] The Masonic Lodge is an ideal setting for those seeking spiritual growth without adhering to institutionalized faiths.

To attract the growing population of those who identify as Spiritual but Not Religious, Freemasonry can emphasize its inclusive and philosophical nature. Rather than focusing on dogma, the Craft encourages members to explore universal spiritual principles through symbolism, personal reflection, and moral development. By offering study groups, discussion forums, and esoteric education focused on self-improvement, meditation, and the pursuit of truth, Lodges can provide a meaningful spiritual experience without the constraints of traditional religion.

Esoteric study plays a crucial role in this spiritual journey within Freemasonry. By engaging with the deeper meanings behind Masonic symbols, rituals and allegories, and other speculative endeavors, members are encouraged to pursue personal spiritual enlightenment. This non-sectarian, introspective approach aligns with the desires of modern men who, while distancing themselves from organized religion, still seek connection with the divine and inner transformation. Freemasonry offers a meaningful path for

102   James Anderson, *The Constitutions of the Free-Masons: Containing the History, Charges, Regulations, &c. of That Most Ancient and Right Worshipful Fraternity. For the Use of the Lodges* (London: printed by William Hunter, for John Senex, and John Hooke, 1723), 50.

such individuals to explore universal truths through both intellectual inquiry and personal reflection.

Continuous Learning

The importance of learning *how* to memorize in early Masonry can be clearly seen in the Schaw Statutes, a set of regulations issued in 1598–1599 by William Schaw, who was the Master of Work and General Warden of the Masonic Lodges in Scotland at the time. These statutes outlined rules and guidelines for the organization and conduct of Masonic lodges in Scotland.

The Schaw Statutes specifically mention the "art of memory" as something that the Warden of the Lodge should test the fellows and apprentices on, according to their vocation.[103]

This reference to the "art of memory" was likely not just about retaining practical knowledge, but rather referred to specific mnemonic techniques and traditions that were prevalent at the time. David Stevenson in *The Origins of Freemasonry* states that this reference demonstrates "the Schaw lodges were at least dabbling in occult and mystical strands of late Renaissance thought."[104]

In monastic environments, texts served as "memoranda, aids to the recreation of the experiential process that links man and God through Christ."[105] This perspective elevated the act of memorization from a mere cognitive exercise to a profound spiritual practice, laying the foundation for what would become Masonic memory techniques.

Central to this practice was the idea that memory is not a passive

103 David Stevenson, *The Origins of Freemasonry: Scotland's Century, 1590–1710* (Cambridge University Press, 1990), 49.

104 Stevenson, *The Origins of Freemasonry*, 50.

105 Janet Coleman, *Ancient and Medieval Memories: Studies in the Reconstruction of the Past* (Cambridge, UK ; New York: Cambridge University Press, 1992), 168.

88

repository of past events, but an active, present-focused mental activity. Janet Coleman tells us, "as with Augustine, for Anselm memory is a mental activity in the present rather than of the past."[106] This concept of active memory engagement was fundamental to monastic meditation, described as "an activation of an already filled memory."[107]

Monastic practitioners used these memory techniques not just for rote memorization, but as a means of deep spiritual engagement. Coleman describes Monastic meditation practices as rumination on "memorized truths, seeking to understand them better, for they are already in the memory."[108] This rumination on memorized texts, particularly Scripture and writings of the Church Fathers, was seen as a path to greater spiritual understanding and closeness to God.

The principles of these memory techniques offer intriguing possibilities for deepening the understanding and practice of Masonic symbolism. Just as monastic practitioners used mental imagery and active memory engagement to contemplate spiritual truths, Masons could apply similar techniques to their symbolic work.

For instance, Masonic symbols like the beehive could be approached through structured memory exercises. Brothers might be guided to visualize the beehive in detail, associating each component with specific Masonic virtues or teachings. This practice of active visualization and association could promote a more profound, personal engagement with the symbol.

Anselm's teaching that thoughts derived from memorial images serve as the words or images that represent the objects of those thoughts is particularly relevant here. By encouraging members to create their own mental imagery and associations with Masonic symbols, Lodges could foster a richer, more individualized understanding of the Craft's allegorical language.

106 Coleman, *Ancient and Medieval Memories*, 168.
107 Coleman, *Ancient and Medieval Memories*, 166.
108 Coleman, *Ancient and Medieval Memories*, 166.

Central to this contemplative memory practice was the use of Corporeal Similitudes—anthropomorphic images placed within memory palaces. Aquinas emphasized their importance, stating that "simple and spiritual impressions easily slip from the mind, unless they be tied as it were to some corporeal image, because human knowledge has a greater hold on sensible objects."[109]

The practice had a profound influence on religious architecture and iconography. Churches were often designed with the art of memory in mind, featuring statues, stained glass windows, and paintings arranged to facilitate memorization and contemplation.[110] These elements served as mnemonic devices for biblical stories, virtues, and spiritual teachings.

The *Ars Memoria* transcended mere technique, becoming a path to moral improvement and spiritual transformation. Practitioners believed that what was memorized became part of one's consciousness, shaping virtues and character. This rich tradition demonstrates how medieval Christians integrated theological concepts, biblical narratives, and moral teachings into a comprehensive system of memory and spiritual development, leaving a lasting impact on Western intellectual and spiritual practices.

The Art of Memory, as exemplified in monastic traditions, offers valuable insights for Masonic Lodges seeking to deepen their exploration of symbols. Just as medieval monks used elaborate mental imagery to internalize spiritual truths, Masons can employ similar techniques to unlock the layers of meaning within Lodge symbols. For instance, the beehive can be approached through a structured memory exercise. Brothers might be guided to visualize the beehive in detail, associating each component—the industrious bees, the hexagonal cells, the golden honey—with specific Masonic virtues

---

109 St. Thomas of Aquinas, *Summa Theologica*, trans. Fathers of the English Dominican Province (London: Benziger Bros., 1947), II-II Q.49.

110 Frances A. Yates, *The Art of Memory* (Chicago: University of Chicago Press, 1966), 51.

or teachings. This practice of active visualization and association, reminiscent of the monastic art of memory, not only aids in retention but also promotes a more profound, personal engagement with the symbol.

Anselm suggests in his *Monologion*, "thoughts formed from memorial images are the representing words or images of the objects of thought."[111] By encouraging members to create their own contemplative study of Masonic symbols, Lodges can foster a richer, more individualized understanding of the Craft's allegorical language, much as medieval monasticism used memory techniques to internalize and contemplate divine truths. This approach aligns with Anselm's view that "the mind beholds itself by remembering itself, then understanding itself and finally loving itself,"[112] a process that can be applied to the contemplation of Masonic symbols.

The Art of Memory offers valuable insights and techniques that Masonic Lodges could explore to enhance their structured educational programs and deepen the understanding of symbolic work among members. Just as medieval monastic practitioners used vivid mental imagery, active memory engagement, and the creation of "corporeal similitudes" to internalize spiritual truths, Masonic education programs could apply similar methods to the contemplation of ritual, symbols, and Masonic teachings. By guiding members through structured memory exercises and visualization techniques focused on key Masonic symbols, ceremonies, and allegories, Lodges could foster a more profound, personal, and transformative engagement with the Craft.

This traditional emphasis on memory as an active, present-focused mental activity, rather than a passive repository of the past, resonates with the Masonic emphasis on self-improvement and moral development. Medieval monasticism used memory techniques as a path to greater spiritual understanding, Masons could

111   Coleman, *Ancient and Medieval Memories*, 156.
112   Coleman, *Ancient and Medieval Memories*, 165.

leverage similar practices within their structured education programs to deepen their own transformative experience within the Craft.

Ultimately, exploring the parallels between the *Ars Memoria* and Masonic symbolism and education offers the potential to revitalize the way Masons approach and internalize the rich allegorical system at the heart of their tradition. By drawing inspiration from these historical memory practices, Masonic Lodges may uncover new avenues for cultivating a more profound, personal, and meaningful engagement with the Craft among their members.

Divided, Never Conquered

A forgotten, but extremely important aspect of Masonic Tradition is the Tower of Babel. The Cooke Manuscript (c. 1450) references the Tower of Babel as part of the broader narrative connecting the origins of geometry and Masonry to ancient biblical traditions. According to this document, the descendants of Noah, particularly those who survived the flood, are credited with preserving and continuing the craft of Masonry. The Tower of Babel, in this context, is presented as a monumental construction based on ancient principles of geometry, symbolically linking it to the knowledge and skills of early Masons. This connection further underscores Masonry's deep historical and divine foundations, tracing its origins to sacred and timeless traditions.

The Tower of Babel stands as a symbol of human ambition—a structure so magnificent, it sought to pierce the heavens. Yet, the story tells us that such a feat could not be allowed to transpire, for it demonstrated the unchecked power of cooperation. The scattering of languages represents the ultimate tool of division, reminding us that the strength of humanity lies in its ability to work together.

This ancient loss of a common language severed our potential to create something of divine magnitude. But what if this unifying force, this shared language, has not been entirely lost? Masonic tradition suggests that the knowledge of such cooperation—of reverence for the Creator and His work—has been preserved. In the secret rituals, signs, and language of the Masons, handed down through generations, we find echoes of that original unity. To truly be a Mason is to recognize the sacred in every space, to see all humans as brethren, and to understand the hand of Divine Providence that guides our actions. The ancient Masons, like those described in *Bearla lagair*, kept a sacred language alive, ensuring that this power to create, to honor the Creator, and to understand one another was not lost but safeguarded for those worthy of the Craft.

This concept of a sacred, preserved language finds a striking parallel in Masonic tradition through what is known as "The Mason's Faculty."[113] Deeply rooted in early Grand Lodge Freemasonry, this notion suggests that Masons possessed a special ability to communicate that transcended the confusion of tongues at Babel.

Anderson's *Constitutions* of 1723 explicitly states that the "Science and Art were both transmitted to latter Ages and distant Climes, notwithstanding the Confusion of Languages or Dialects," giving rise to "the Masons Faculty and ancient universal Practice of conversing without speaking."[114] This faculty wasn't merely a set of recognition signs, but a sophisticated primordial language of symbols.[115]

113 James Anderson, *The Constitutions of the Free-Masons: Containing the History, Charges, Regulations, &c. of That Most Ancient and Right Worshipful Fraternity. For the Use of the Lodges* (London: printed by William Hunter, for John Senex, and John Hooke, 1723), 5.

114 Anderson, *Constitutions of the Free-Masons* (1723), 5.

115 Shawn Eyer, "The Essential Secrets of Masonry: Insight from an American Masonic Oration of 1734," in *Exploring Early Grand Lodge Freemasonry: Studies in Honor of the Tricentennial of the Establishment of the Grand Lodge of England*, ed. Christopher B. Murphy and Shawn Eyer (Washington, D.C.: Plumbstone

A vivid account from 1735, likely delivered by Provincial Grand Master Joseph Laycock, elaborates on this concept:

> Their Design and End in building this prodigious Tower (as we suppose) was not only for establishing a Name, but also to fix a Centre of Unity and Correspondence, to which they might, upon any Occasion, repair.... But their Designs running counter to the Purpose of the Almighty, what they endeavoured to avoid, he miraculously brought about by the Confusion of Tongues, which gave Origin to the Masons antient Practice of conversing without speaking, by means of proper Signals expressive of their Ideas.[116]

This "faculty" was believed to be more than just a means of secret recognition. It was seen as a way to preserve and transmit complex ideas—a remnant of the universal language that existed before Babel.[117] The Mason's Faculty, then, stands as a testament to the enduring power of unity and shared understanding. It suggests that while languages may divide, the essence of human cooperation and divine connection can still be preserved through carefully guarded traditions and practices. In this light, Masonry becomes not just a craft, but a keeper of an ancient, sacred mode of communication—a living link to the unity that existed before the Tower of Babel fell.

This "faculty" was believed to be more than just a means of secret recognition. It was seen as a way to preserve and transmit complex ideas—a remnant of the universal language that existed before Babel. The Mason's Faculty, then, stands as a testament to the enduring power of unity and shared understanding. It suggests that

Academic, 2017), 181.

116   William Smith, *The Book M: Or, Masonry Triumphant* (Newcastle upon Tyne: Printed by Leonard Umfreville and Company, 1736), 1:19.

117   Christopher B. Murphy, "The Mason's Faculty and the Language of Adam: An Untrod Path of Inquiry," *The Plumbline* 25, no. 4 (2018): 4–5.

while languages may divide, the essence of human cooperation and divine connection can still be preserved through carefully guarded traditions and practices. In this light, Masonry becomes not just a craft, but a keeper of an ancient, sacred mode of communication—a living link to the unity that existed before the Tower of Babel fell.

This idea of preserved, sacred communication finds further resonance in the research of A.T. Sinclair, who examined Bearla Lagair—the cryptic tongue spoken by Irish stonemasons to communicate with one another in secrecy, much like the Mason's Faculty. Apprentices were required to learn this hidden language as part of their craft, ensuring that the knowledge and methods of the trade could be transmitted without interference from outsiders.[118]

Sinclair also draws attention to the tinkers' language, *Shelta*, a similarly veiled form of communication used by nomadic Irish craftsmen. Both *Bearla Lagair* and *Shelta* share roots in ancient Irish dialects, with words often reversed or disguised.[119] These secret languages allowed these communities to preserve their skills, histories, and even their very identities across centuries.

By examining these linguistic traditions, Sinclair uncovered a living, yet often overlooked, legacy of sacred communication. These languages were not merely practical tools for their respective trades but embodied a deeper connection to an ancient, almost mythic past—just as the Mason's Faculty claimed to do.

In both the Mason's Faculty and the *Bearla Lagair*, we see a shared effort to preserve something profound: the ability to communicate beyond the limitations of language, to pass down sacred knowledge untainted by the lapse of time. Whether in the halls of Freemasonry or the workshops of Irish stonemasons, this ancient faculty serves as a bridge between the past and present, a testament to the human desire for unity and understanding that transcends

118   A. T. Sinclair, "The Secret Language of Masons and Tinkers," *The Journal of American Folklore* 22, no. 86 (1909): 354.
119   Sinclair, "The Secret Language of Masons and Tinkers," 359.

the boundaries imposed by history.

In this light, the Mason's Faculty is not simply a symbolic tool but part of a broader tradition of using hidden languages to maintain sacred knowledge, echoing through both mythical and practical realms. Whether among builders, tinkers, or even Freemasons, the preservation of such sacred languages reflects an enduring connection to a time when words were not yet barriers but pathways to divine unity.

Masonry, at its core, is about the impermanence of all things; most especially, it is about the impermanence of us. Every day—whether we know it or not—we are greeted by "striking" instances of mortality that "remind us of our approaching fate."[120] For example, you may recall the commonly told story of triumphant Roman soldiers who, upon returning in victory, were reminded by a companion or slave that life was fleeting and death imminent.

This is to commend a wise and serious truth: Mankind used to reflect frequently on the inescapable reach of Death through the contemplation of symbols. Many contemporary Masons still do this by filling their offices, studies, or workspaces with Tracing Boards, Working Tools, and other symbolic representations of the Fraternity.

Success Criteria

A historical perspective is useful, but Masonic education must be viewed through the practicality of modern applications. For example, implementations of structured Masonic educational programs must focus on andragogy—the particular techniques that facilitate

---

120 Preston, *Illustrations of Masonry: A Grand Gala in Honour of Free Masonry, Held at the Crown and Anchor Tavern, in the Strand,* 242–43.

learning in adults rather than children—as a practice.[121]

Modern implementations of Masonic education programs must consider the specific needs and characteristics of adult learners. Malcolm Knowles, a pioneer in adult education theory, identified six key assumptions about adult learners that are particularly relevant to Masonic education. These include:

- The need to know why they are learning something,
- A self-concept of being responsible for their own decisions,
- The role of learners' experiences,
- Readiness to learn,
- Orientation to learning, and
- Motivation[122]

For instance, Masons are likely to be more engaged in learning rituals or Masonic history if they understand how this knowledge will enhance their Masonic experience or contribute to their personal growth. This aligns with Knowles' first assumption about adults' need to know. Furthermore, the rich life experiences that adult Masons bring to their lodges can be leveraged as a resource for learning, reflecting Knowles' third assumption about the role of learners' experiences.[123]

Training mentors in adult education techniques and providing them with standardized materials aligns with the need to create an effective learning environment for adults. The educator's role is to "engage in a process of mutual inquiry with [adult learners] rather

121 Eric Beeson, "Andragogy" in *The SAGE Encyclopedia of Educational Research, Measurement, and Evaluation* (Thousand Oaks, Calif.: SAGE Publications, Inc, 2018).

122 Malcolm S. Knowles, Elwood F. Holton III, and Richard A. Swanson, *The Adult Learner: The Definitive Classic in Adult Education and Human Resource Development* (Burlington, Ma.: Butterworth-Heinemann, 2005), 64–68.

123 Knowles, et al., *The Adult Learner*, 65.

than to transmit his or her knowledge to them and then evaluate their conformity to it."[124] This approach respects the Mason's need for self-direction and leverages their life experiences.

The incorporation of goal-setting and progress tracking for both mentor and mentee addresses the adult learner's need for self-direction and motivation. It's been suggested that the "most potent motivators are internal pressures (the desire for increased job satisfaction, self-esteem, quality of life, and the like)."[125] By setting personal goals and tracking progress, Masons can tap into these internal motivators.

Structured reading lists for each degree, updated with contemporary scholarship, can address the adult learner's need to know and readiness to learn. By curating lists that balance classic texts with modern scholarly works, this approach can help Masons understand both the historical context and current relevance of Masonic knowledge.

Online learning modules covering foundational topics represent a significant modernization of Masonic education. These e-learning platforms, similar to the United Grand Lodge of England's "Solomon" program, can address multiple andragogical principles. They allow for self-directed learning, catering to adults' need for autonomy. Interactive elements and assessments can provide immediate feedback, supporting the adult learner's orientation to learning. Adults are motivated "to the extent that they perceive that learning will help them perform tasks or deal with problems that they confront in their life situations."[126] By providing practical, applicable knowledge through these modules, Masonic education can directly address this motivation.

These modern implementations can be tailored to suit the needs and resources of individual Grand Lodges or even local lodges. The

124 Knowles, et al., *The Adult Learner*, 40.
125 Knowles, et al., *The Adult Learner*, 68.
126 Knowles, et al., *The Adult Learner*, 67.

key is to create a comprehensive, engaging, and accessible educational program that caters to the diverse learning styles and interests of modern Masons while maintaining the depth and richness of Masonic tradition.

By combining these approaches—personalized mentorship, curated reading lists, and leveraging technology for online learning—Masonic education can become more structured, consistent, and adaptable. This multi-faceted approach ensures that the core principles of Masonic education, as outlined by scholars like Speth over a century ago, are preserved and enhanced for future generations.

Speth's approach naturally lends itself to a tiered learning system. He categorizes his recommended readings as:

- Absolutely Indispensable
- Strongly Recommended
- Recommended
- Additional[127]

This tiered system can be adapted to create a modern curriculum:

- Tier 1:
  Essential Masonic knowledge (history, symbolism, ritual)
- Tier 2:
  Advanced Masonic studies (philosophy, comparative religion, esoteric traditions)
- Tier 3:
  Specialized research and contribution to Masonic scholarship

Speth encourages Masons to progress from being students to contributors, stating that after mastering the basics, a Mason should

---

127 Speth, "A Masonic Curriculum," 119–20.

"strive to add to our joint knowledge."[128] Speth is certainly invoking the beehive here. Through the industrious labor of each bee, working together to produce honey (or, in the Masonic context, wisdom), Speth is advocating for a similar ethos of continuous learning and collective contribution within the fraternity.

There is, perhaps, an invisible line between 'routine' and 'ritual,' or at least a point at which it is clear—like a Catholic transubstantiation—that a change has occurred. It seems to relate to the importance or meaning we associate with the recurring task. It is not always clear to everyone where this line is, but it is clear that the vehicle by which it is traversed is *intent*.

Intent is such an important principle to teach. Mindfulness became a buzzword in the 2010s, and it got used and abused to the point of meaninglessness. This is unfortunate, because to be truly present is to be meditative. It honestly can be that simple. The contemplative Lodge is created by contemplation.

Pay attention to your steps as you move about the Lodge room.

- Are you slow and purposeful and aware of every action?
- Can you apply mathematical principles to movement?

A Mason should be encouraged in all situations to raise his awareness. This allows us to act in accordance with the Biblical Patriarchs who, upon being summoned by Divinity, often responded with "Here I am."[129] The spiritually present man is aware of what is being asked of him in every endeavor and fully invests in the work. We are building a Temple to the Most High that may never be completed, and no task is more worthy of our time.

It is frequently said of the degrees that they provide extreme amounts of information. The most common simile provided is that it's like drinking from a firehose. And yet, due to the operational

128 Speth, "A Masonic Curriculum," 119.
129 Genesis 22:1, 22:11, 31:11, 37:13, 46:2, Exodus 3:4.

necessities of many Lodges (e.g., Stated Communication can only occur when opened on the Master Mason Degree), the business of proficiency takes priority over any actual reflection. I contend that reflection leads to proficiency.

In many Lodges, brothers compose and deliver reflective papers (1500–2000 words) on the most meaningful part of the degree. Initiates choose from any emblem, lecture, remark, or piece of the Forms and Ceremonies. Imagine if you requested this of every initiate in every degree! A Lodge could collect all the papers, arrange them as a document, then print an annual bulletin. What better way to preserve the intellectual history of our Lodges and give the Grand Historian something worthy to preserve for posterity.

If the initiates of the Lodge immediately see their place in the hive and feel they are making a contribution to the stock of knowledge, they are more likely to want to contribute in other ways. We value things that challenge us. A meeting where we introduce all the grand people, talk about the bills calendar, and then focus on the next Shrine or Scottish Rite club meeting is sure to encourage none to attend. But these problems are not unrelated because imagine how strong the Scottish Rite club will be when every new applicant is coming to the appendant bodies with a mind for reflection and writing. It benefits every facet of the Masonic experience to force reflective practice in written form after each degree of the initiatic experience.

Intellectual curiosity should be encouraged and celebrated in every single Masonic lodge. This is the whole game—*I think of something I want to know about, I find someone who knows about it, and I learn from them.* Masonry fails when Masons think it's over. Or rather, when Masons believe that attending a degree is the same as receiving a degree. The receiving comes much later, or— if we're being honest of many Masons—not at all. After all, there are still Masons who believe that the 'secrets of Freemasonry' are handshakes and passwords. These men are akin to Ruffians—False

Brethren—desirous to obtain something they clearly are not worthy to possess, and angry when others seem to have found something they do not comprehend. A culture of learning is the rising tide that lifts all boats. Imagine knowing that each year, without fail, every member will have the ability to deepen his understanding of the moral lessons of the Craft. The lessons of the Lodge thereby become Corporeal Similitudes— living entities that return, grow, evolve, and transform.

Masonic teachings aren't trading cards. There's no benefit to trying to catch all the titles. There is, however, real benefit *in* the work and labor. We believe the authors of the work chose their words carefully and deliberately. Freemasonry is the unending and purposeful improvement of the self. It isn't supposed to be easy.

Implementing structured educational programs in Freemasonry requires balancing historical traditions with modern educational methods. By adapting historical models like Speth's curriculum and incorporating successful contemporary approaches, Lodges can create robust educational programs that cater to both new initiates and experienced members, fostering a culture of continuous learning and intellectual growth within the Craft.

Modern Freemasonry's 300th anniversary is now behind us, and prior to that we have another 300 years of history. Six centuries of tradition depend upon us—and empower us. Reinvigorating our educational programs is crucial for maintaining the relevance and vitality of the fraternity. By implementing structured, tiered learning systems, we can ensure that the light of Masonic knowledge continues to shine brightly for future generations.

Like the industrious bees, Masons must work collectively to build and maintain their stock of knowledge. The Lodge, akin to the hive, should be a place where every member contributes to and benefits from shared wisdom.

The tiered structure of Masonic degrees aligns naturally with the organized layers of the beehive, providing a framework for progressive learning. From the newly initiated Entered Apprentice to the experienced Master Mason, each level offers unique opportunities for growth and contribution. Education built on this system, reminiscent of Speth's categorizations, ensures a path of continuous learning for all members.

By incorporating elements of the Art of Memory and other historical educational practices, Lodges can deepen their members' engagement with Masonic symbolism and philosophy. These techniques, adapted for modern use, bridge the gap between ancient wisdom and contemporary learning methods.

Ultimately, robust Masonic education is essential for restoring balance between the Operative and Speculative aspects of the Craft. As we approach Freemasonry's Quadricentennial, a renewed focus on learning will ensure that Lodges remain vibrant centers of intellectual and spiritual growth, preserving and evolving the rich heritage of the fraternity for future generations.

7

Building the Inner Temple: Esoteric Practice

MANY MASONS will be familiar with the idea that Free-masonry is "intent upon making good men better men and thus a good world a better world."[130] This is a false-hood because Masonry cannot do that. Such transformation *must* be an act of one's own free will and accord. If the Lodge is to have any role in this process whatsoever, it is primarily to serve as a voluntary accountability system for the self improvement of each brother. Thaddeus Mason Harris has repeatedly charged millions of Masons to remember their promises to:

---

130   Rex R. Hutchens, Ronald A. Seale, and Arturo de Hoyos, *A Bridge To Light: A Study In Masonic Ritual & Philosophy*, 4th edition (Washington, D.C.: The Supreme Council of the Scottish Rite, 2021), 143.

remind [every Brother], in the most tender manner, of his fail-
ings, and aid his reformation: To vindicate his character when
wrongfully traduced; and to suggest in his behalf the most candid,
favourable, and palliating circumstances, even when his conduct
is justly reprehended. That the world may observe how Masons
love one another.[131]

In this way, each member is duty-bound to assist all mankind in
the kindest possible manner. Here is a way, through active love
and kindness, for the lodge to create its own legacy, posterity, and
sanctity. True brotherhood will develop.

Masons can cultivate a mindset that integrates the lessons of
the lodge into their daily lives. We know through contemporary
psychology that "a growth mindset, then, creates a context in which
you can fully understand [the hard work you are doing] is growing
your brain, growing your talent."[132] This involves viewing challenges
as opportunities for growth, approaching tasks with diligence and
purpose and maintaining a commitment to ethical behavior and
self-improvement. The true Mason sees his inner life as the unfinished Temple, requiring regular attention and care. In the same way
that the physical Lodge building is a place of order and purpose, the
Inner Temple is a space where Masons can cultivate the very highest
virtues and aspirations.[133] Wilmshurst incisively cuts through the
din in *The Meaning of Masonry*:

Each of us is the sepulchre in which the smitten Master is in-
terred. If we know it not, it is a further sign of our benightedness.
At the centre of ourselves, deeper than any dissecting-knife can

131 Thaddeus Mason Harris, *Constitutions of the Ancient and
Honourable Fraternity of Free and Accepted Masons* (Worcester,
Mass.: Isaiah Thomas, 1792), 174.

132 Howard Burton, *Mindsets: Growing Your Brain* (Toronto, Canada:
Open Agenda Publishing, 2020), 34.

133 1 Corinthians 3:16.

reach or than any physical investigation can fathom, lies buried the 'vital and immortal principle,' the 'glimmering ray' that affiliates us to the Divine Centre of all life, and that is never wholly extinguished however evil or imperfect our lives may be. We are the grave of the Master. The lost guiding light is buried at the centre of ourselves.[134]

And so it seems that Masons have always been called to inner work. The consistent effort of incorporating contemplation, meditation, study, and reflection—much like the ongoing labor of bees—will truly demonstrate the strength of Wisdom in time.

The beehive, as a symbol of productive labor and collective wisdom, is also a metaphor for the inner work of Freemasonry. Just as bees tirelessly gather nectar and transform it into honey, Masons are called to gather knowledge and experience, distilling it into wisdom through dedicated spiritual practice.

The rich symbolism of Freemasonry provides fertile ground for meditative practice. By focusing on symbols such as the beehive, the square and compasses, or the trowel, Masons can quiet their minds and gain deeper insights into the spiritual significance of these emblems.

For example, a Mason might meditate on the beehive by visualizing its structure, contemplating how each bee's role contributes to the whole. This practice can lead to insights about one's place within the Lodge and the broader community, fostering a sense of interconnectedness and shared purpose.

Guided reflections can help Masons internalize the lessons of the beehive. Consider the following contemplation:

Visualize yourself as a bee within the hive of your Lodge. How do your actions contribute to the collective wisdom and strength of

---

134   Walter Leslie Wilmshurst, *The Meaning of Masonry* (San Francisco: Plumbstone, 2007), 55.

the fraternity? In what ways can you embody the industriousness, cooperation, and purpose-driven nature of the bee in your daily life and Masonic practice?

Such reflections encourage Masons to apply the symbolic lessons of the beehive to their personal and spiritual development.

Collective Growth

To truly understand the deeper meanings of Masonic symbolism, Masons should engage with esoteric texts that align with Freemasonry's teachings. Works on Hermeticism, Kabbalah, and alchemy can provide valuable insights, enriching one's spiritual practice and understanding of Masonic ritual.

For instance, W. Kirk MacNulty has described the portions of the second degree as the Hermetic principle of correspondence ("as above, so below").[135] Such a contemplation would certainly deepen the Mason's understanding of how the microcosm of personal development relates to the macrocosm of universal laws, a concept often reflected in Masonic teachings. Additionally, MacNulty has also described the Craft degrees within a Kabbalistic cosmology.[136] We do not need to go outside the Fraternity to find connections to the best pieces of Western Esoteric Traditions. We do, however, need to engage with Masonic literature.

Classic Masonic literature offers profound interpretations of symbols and teachings. Works like Anderson's *Constitutions*, Preston's *Illustrations*, Cross's *Monitor*, and others provide a solid foundation for spiritual inquiry within the Masonic tradition. By engaging with such texts, Masons can deepen their understanding

135 W. Kirk MacNulty, *The Way of the Craftsman: Deluxe Edition* (Washington, D.C.: Plumbstone, 2017), 34.
136 MacNulty, *The Way of the Craftsman*, 43.

of the Craft's esoteric dimensions and apply these insights to their inner work.

Spiritual Work

Just as bees work tirelessly to produce honey, Masons should develop a regular practice of inner work. This might involve setting aside time each day for meditation, study, or reflection on Masonic principles. Consistency is key; even short daily practices can yield significant spiritual growth over time.

The beehive demonstrates a perfect balance between individual effort and collective purpose. Similarly, Masons must strive to balance their inner spiritual work with their outer obligations and service. This equilibrium ensures that personal growth translates into meaningful action in the world.

The alchemical process of transmuting base metals into gold serves as an apt metaphor for the inner work of Freemasonry. Through dedicated study, meditation, and self-reflection, Masons can transform their baser instincts into higher virtues, producing the "gold" of wisdom and enlightenment. This process is not unlike the bees' transformation of nectar into honey. It requires patience, consistent effort, and a willingness to engage with challenging material. As Charles Leslie reminds, "Tho' the passage be difficult, the further we trace it, the easier it will become."[137]

The wisdom gained through inner work should not be hoarded but shared, both within the Lodge and in the broader community.

137 Charles Leslie, "A Vindication of Masonry, and its Excellency Demonstrated in a Discourse at the Consecration of the Lodge Vernon Kilwinning, on May 15, 1741, by Charles Leslie, M.A. Master-Mason and Member of that Lodge." In *The Free Masons Pocket-companion* (Edinburgh: Printed by Auld, and Smellie, and sold at their Printing House, Morocco's Close, Lawn-Market, M,DCC,LXV [1765]), 162.

Just as bees share the honey they produce, Masons are encouraged to share their insights and knowledge, contributing to the collective growth of the Craft.

This sharing might take the form of presenting papers in Lodge, mentoring younger Masons, or applying Masonic principles in one's professional and personal life. By doing so, Masons fulfill their duty to spread the light of wisdom and virtue. Through consistent effort in meditation, study, and reflection, Masons can produce the sweet honey of wisdom, enriching their own lives and contributing to the collective enlightenment of the fraternity. As we engage in this inner work, we honor the legacy of those who came before us and prepare the way for future generations of seekers.

PART IV

Restoring Harmony in the Lodge

8

Operational Excellence
as a Foundation
for Speculative Growth

HERETOFORE we have explored the lasting emblematic meaning of the beehive in Masonic tradition. Throughout esoteric traditions, the beehive has served as a powerful emblem of industry, cooperation, and collective wisdom. As we turn our attention to the practical aspects of Lodge management, it is fitting that we once again look to the beehive for guidance and inspiration.

The concept of the Lodge as a hive is more than mere allegory; it provides a robust framework for understanding and improving the function of our Masonic institutions. Just as a beehive operates with remarkable efficiency, purpose, and harmony, so should our Lodges strive for a balance of operational excellence and spiritual depth.

In the natural world, the beehive's structure and organization serve a higher purpose: the sustenance of the colony and the production of honey. Similarly, the operational aspects of our Lodges should not be ends in themselves, but rather the means by which we create an environment conducive to personal growth, brotherly love, and the pursuit of Masonic light.

Too much attention in Masonry is directed into the practical considerations of Lodge management. We must keep in mind that our goal is not simply to run efficient meetings or balance ledgers. Rather, we seek to create a harmonious and purposeful Masonic experience that allows each brother to contribute meaningfully and grow spiritually. By emulating the beehive's efficiency and cooperation in our day-to-day functioning, we lay the groundwork for profound speculative experiences.

Here, we will ideate how Lodges can streamline their operations, reduce administrative distractions, and focus on what truly matters—ritual, education, and the cultivation of Masonic virtues. We will endeavor to strike a delicate balance between the practical necessities of running a Lodge and the higher calling of Freemasonry as a transformative, initiatic tradition.

Let us remember that the ultimate aim of our labors, like those of the bees, is to produce something sweet and nourishing—not mere honey, but the sublime wisdom and brotherly affection that are the hallmarks of a truly harmonious Lodge. By tending carefully to the structure and operation of our speculative hive, we create the conditions for the *mysteries of godliness* to unfold, and the precious nectar of Masonic experience can flow abundantly.

The beehive's remarkable efficiency stems from its well-defined structure and the clear roles of its inhabitants. Each bee knows its purpose and works tirelessly towards the common good. Our Masonic Lodges can learn much from this model of cooperative labor and purposeful organization.

In a beehive, the queen, workers, and drones each have distinct roles that contribute to the hive's overall success. Similarly, a well-structured Lodge leadership team is crucial for efficient operations.

The Worshipful Master, like the queen bee, sets the tone and direction for the Lodge. However, unlike the queen bee, the Master's role is not to dominate but to guide and inspire. The Master should:

- Clearly articulate the Lodge's vision and goals for the year, which must be to perpetuate true Freemasonry
- Delegate responsibilities effectively to other officers and committees
- Ascend to the charge of his installation
- Ensure that all aspects of Lodge operations align with Masonic principles and traditions

The Tyler, Marshall, Secretary, and Treasurer can be likened to specialized worker bees, each with crucial roles:

- Tyler: Focuses on membership development and future planning
- Marshall: Oversees fellowship activities and Lodge hospitality
- Secretary: Manages communication and record-keeping
- Treasurer: Ensures financial stability and transparency

Other officers and committee chairs represent the diverse workforce of the hive, each contributing their unique skills and efforts to the Lodge's success.

Like a beehive preparing future queens, Lodges must actively develop their future leaders. Thankfully, Masonic leadership programs are plentiful and most Grand Lodges offer training materials and opportunities to anyone interested in these areas. Some additional thoughts to consider:

- Experiment for a decade or so with a structured yet non-progressive officer line. Brothers can still learn multiple parts without needing the stress of a new Master every year.
- Encourage experienced Past Masters to mentor newer officers or fill vacant chairs without the obligation of advancing.
- Provide leadership training opportunities, both within and outside the Lodge.
- Create a culture where knowledge is freely shared, ensuring continuity in Lodge operations.

By growing a garden of shared responsibility and continuous learning, Lodges can harvest smooth transitions of leadership and maintain operational excellence over time.

Resource Management

As bees must efficiently manage their resources of nectar and pollen, Lodges must be wise stewards of their financial resources. This involves not only appropriate budgeting, but also involves transparency in financial stewardship.

If you want to know what an organization values, observe where they actually spend their money. When financially planning for the year, develop an annual budget that reflects the Lodge's priorities and Masonic values.

- Mindfully allocate funds not just for operational needs, but for education, charity, and member development.
- Invest in the Lodge's future by setting aside funds for long-term projects and building maintenance.
- Consider creating separate funds for specific purposes (e.g., charity, education, building preservation).

The Lodge treasurer is duly obligated to "keep a just and true account" of all transactions and only to pay expenses with "consent of the Brethren."[138] Even when expenses are approved at stated meetings, many of the members do not fully understand the actual financial machinations necessary to Lodge functions. To improve this, provide regular, clear financial reports to the membership and implement checks and balances in financial processes to ensure accountability. Conduct annual audits and share results with the membership. This will make the long-term missions of the Lodge accessible and understandable to all stakeholders.

Finally, as you grow new Masonic leaders, educate officers and members on financial best practices and Masonic financial regulations. By managing finances with transparency and purpose, Lodges can build trust among members and ensure resources are used effectively to support both operational needs and Masonic growth.

Many Lodges attempt to alternate between business-oriented meetings and educational or degree meetings when possible. This seems to eventually devolve into degrees and business with very little education or spiritual engagement. This seems to violate the obligation supposedly undertaken by Lodge Masters never to close a Lodge "without giving a lecture, or some section or part of a lecture, for the instruction of the Lodge."[139]

This inconvenient matter is often brushed off because the lectures of Masonry may be thought of as including balloting procedures and the ceremony for opening and closing a Lodge.[140] In other words, many are happy to request full credit when doing minimal

---

138 William Morgan, *Illustrations of Masonry, by One of the Fraternity, Who Has Devoted Thirty Years to the Subject: With an Appendix, Containing a Key to the Higher Degrees of Freemasonry; by a Member of the Craft* (Cincinnati: Matthew Gardiner, 1826), 14.

139 Malcom C. Duncan, *Duncan's Masonic Ritual and Monitor* (New York: Dick & Fitzgerald, 1866), 190.

140 William Preston, *Illustrations of Masonry*, 2nd ed. (London: Printed for J. Wilkie, No. 71. St. Paul's Church Yard, 1775), 47.

work. To better embody the spirit of this charge, incorporate brief educational segments into business meetings to maintain focus on Masonic principles. Additionally, try to close each meeting with a short period of reflection or discussion on the evening's Masonic work.

By managing time effectively in Lodge meetings, we create space for both necessary operations and meaningful Masonic experiences. This balance ensures that every gathering contributes to the growth of the Lodge and its members.

Efficient time management in Lodge meetings mirrors the precision and purpose seen in a beehive. By adopting these practices, Lodges can create an environment where administrative necessities are addressed swiftly and efficiently, leaving ample time for the truly transformative aspects of Freemasonry—ritual, education, and brotherhood. Efficiency in a beehive is partly due to the optimization of necessary tasks. Lodges can apply this principle to their administrative functions.

While preserving the timeless nature of our Craft, Lodges can leverage modern tools to enhance efficiency. However, it is difficult in a book of this nature to dictate how that might be done because any technologies are obsoleted as soon as they are adopted. Additionally, any such use would need to be done in accordance with the Grand Lodge to which the Lodge is beholden. There are some areas where, to the extent possible, the Lodge will want to get creative:

- Adopt digital systems for membership records and dues collection
- Utilize secure cloud storage for important documents and archives
- Implement email newsletters and private social media groups for improved communication
- Consider virtual meeting platforms for committee work and officer meetings

Distribution of labor is key in a beehive, and it should be in a Lodge as well. Create clear, yet broad, job descriptions for each officer and committee role. Form task-specific committees for events, charity work, and education programs rather than standing committees that do not meet with any frequency. This will encourage newer members to take on small responsibilities, fostering engagement and developing future leaders.

The task allocation should be flexible. The system works if you work it. As such, Lodge leadership could regularly review and adjust task allocation to prevent burnout and ensure equitable distribution of work. By streamlining administrative processes and effectively delegating tasks, Lodges can reduce the burden on any single member and create more time for meaningful Masonic work.

Administrative Efficiency

In a beehive, every action serves a purpose, contributing to the colony's survival and prosperity. Similarly, Masonic Lodges must strive to eliminate distractions and focus on activities that truly embody and advance our core values.

To streamline Lodge operations and refocus on core Masonic values, Lodges should conduct a thorough audit of their current practices. The purpose of this audit is fourfold:

- To review all regular activities, committees, and events
- To assess each activity's alignment with Masonic principles and the Lodge's stated goals
- To evaluate the time, resources, and energy required for each activity
- To gather feedback from members on the perceived value of various Lodge functions

Every Lodge is unique because it has unique members who come to the events with unique expectations. Therefore it is important to develop your own set of criteria to determine which activities truly serve the Lodge's Masonic mission. That said, some suggestions include:

- Masonic relevance: Does the activity directly relate to Masonic teachings, symbols, or traditions?
- Member engagement: Does it actively involve and benefit a significant portion of the membership?
- Personal growth: Does it contribute to the moral, intellectual, or spiritual development of members?
- Community impact: Does it positively represent Freemasonry to the wider community?
- Resource efficiency: Is the return in Masonic value proportional to the resources invested?

Activities that score low on these criteria should be carefully reconsidered and potentially eliminated or restructured. When it comes to recurring Lodge activities and customs—sometimes erroneously referred to as 'traditions'—there are no sacred cows. Nothing lasts forever; all temples are inevitably destroyed except for one: the unfinished temple whose construction is the only goal.

Rather than filling the calendar with numerous events, focus on creating fewer, but more significant experiences. Anderson provides an excellent historical basis for discussing the importance of quality over quantity in Masonic gatherings. In Anderson's description of the founding of the Grand Lodge in 1717, he states:

> They and some old Brothers met at the said Apple-Tree, and having put into the Chair the oldest Master Mason (now the Master of a Lodge) they constituted themselves a GRAND LODGE *pro Tempore* in Due Form, and forthwith revived the Quarterly Com-

munication of the Officers of Lodges (call'd the Grand Lodge) resolv'd to hold the Annual ASSEMBLY and Feast, and then to chuse [sic] a GRAND MASTER from among themselves, till they should have the Honour of a Noble Brother at their Head.[141]

Note that our early brethren chose to meet quarterly, not out of a lack of desire for fellowship, but to ensure that each gathering was a significant and memorable event. The Assembly and Feast was an annual occurrence, highlighting its importance and special nature. This approach ensured that when Masons did gather, it was for a purpose and with great anticipation. In our modern Lodges, we can apply this principle by:

* Focusing on creating fewer, but more significant events that brothers eagerly anticipate
* Ensuring that each meeting or gathering has a clear purpose and offers meaningful content
* Investing time and resources into making each event special, much like the Assembly and Feast of old.

By emphasizing quality over quantity, we create Masonic experiences that are truly impactful and memorable. This approach not only respects the time and commitment of our members but also heightens the significance of our gatherings, making them truly special occasions for Masonic labor and fellowship.

141 James Anderson, *The New Book of Constitutions of the Antient and Honourable Fraternity of Free and Accepted Masons. Containing Their History, Charges, Regulations, &c. Collected and Digested by Order of The Grand Lodge from Their Old Records, Faithful Traditions and Lodge-Books, for the Use of the Lodges* (London: Printed for Brothers Cæsar Ward and Richard Chandler, Booksellers, at the Ship Without Temple-Bar; and Sold at Their Shops in Coney-Street, York, and at Scarborough-Spaw, 1738), 109.

Just as early Grand Lodge brethren understood the value of anticipation and preparation in making their quarterly and annual gatherings significant, we too should strive to make each Lodge event an occasion that Brothers look forward to with excitement and leave feeling enriched and inspired. This can be accomplished any number of ways, and you are probably already doing some of them:

- Develop in-depth educational programs that explore Masonic philosophy and symbolism
- Plan degree ceremonies that are meticulously prepared and profoundly delivered
- Organize retreats or workshops focused on personal development and Masonic teachings
- Create opportunities for genuine fellowship and brotherly bonding
- Encouraging depth over frequency in Lodge gatherings

Do not feel guilty over the need to reduce the frequency of activities; as long as the tradeoff is higher quality activities when they do happen. Allocate more time in meetings for substantive discussions and Masonic education, and encourage members to spend time between meetings in personal study and reflection. While some might see this as 'Masonic homework,' it could be gamified. Each meeting the Master asks a trivia question and whomever answers correctly wins a Grand Master's pin. You would have a seemingly infinite prize pool!

Redefining Operative Work

While we are not called on to build physical cathedrals as we once were, the concept of 'Operative' Masonry can be reimagined for the modern era. There are many practical skills that are taught in Lodges. Lodge operations build Operative masons, so to speak. Organize workshops on public speaking, leadership, and interpersonal communication. Additionally, you could offer seminars on personal finance, time management, and other life skills. Host events that provide training in Lodge management, ritual performance, and Masonic education techniques.

These practical skills not only benefit individual members but also contribute to the overall strength and capability of the Lodge. This then naturally extends to the larger geographic community.

The local community needs to be connected to the Lodge. If possible, engage in local community improvement projects—viewing them as modern cathedral-building—or develop partnerships with local charities or educational institutions. The Fraternity thrives when it looks forward to the unbuilt future.

Organize skills-based volunteering where members can apply their professional expertise to community needs. Does anyone in the Lodge know a Physical Therapist or a Personal Trainer? These professionals could be used for the benefit of all, especially if a program or event could be scheduled that focuses on healthy aging practices. The whole Fraternity should strive to live long enough to receive 60+ year membership awards.

Men's style and fashion change frequently, but many attire decisions are actually based in etiquette and decorum. For this reason, style and attire conversations are incredibly useful. For example, many contemporary Freemasons do not know how to tie a bowtie, nor what hat pairs appropriately with his attire in the East. Presentations on this topic for young professionals would help increase traffic to the Lodge. By reframing community service as a form of Operative Masonry, we connect our practical efforts to our speculative teachings on building a better world.

Speculative Integration

When Lodge operation becomes streamlined and efficient, Lodges must prioritize the philosophical and spiritual aspects of Freemasonry. Carl H. Claudy told us almost a century ago there is, "one thing and only one thing a Masonic Lodge can give its members which they can get nowhere else in the world. *That one thing is Masonry.*"[142] Freemasonry remains a moral and social system of perpetual value, as long as it remains true to Freemasonry.

Many attempts have been made over the years to create a standardized education system for Freemasons. The reason this has repeatedly fallen short of the mark is because Freemasonry is too big to contain and reduce in any meaningful way. Imagine if every college marching band was forced to do the same halftime show? The rudiments would still be there, but the Art would be gone. Such displays would be like the porcelain doll in your grandmother's attic: beautiful, fragile, and ultimately of little utility. The structure of the curriculum, rather than the content is what is ultimately important. Additionally, Masons can integrate educational moments into regular business meetings, connecting administrative topics to Masonic principles.

Establish a Lodge library and encourage regular book discussions or study groups. Add new titles to the Library as they are released and cultivate true Masonic knowledge. The value of the institution is longevity, and you cannot achieve optimism for the future if you ignore or dismiss your history.

In every gathering of Freemasons, there must be a brief presentation or discussion that delves into a topic related to Freemasonry, allowing members to explore the depths of their craft and its teachings. These moments provide an opportunity for brothers to

142   Carl H. Claudy, *The Master's Book*. Washington, D.C.: The Temple Publishers, 1935), 18, emphasis in original.

share their personal insights and reflections on how Masonry has influenced their lives, fostering a sense of camaraderie and mutual understanding among the brethren.

To further enhance the Masonic experience, lodges should consider organizing debates or panel discussions that focus on various aspects of Freemasonry. By inviting members with diverse perspectives to participate, these events can facilitate a rich exchange of ideas and opinions, ultimately leading to a more comprehensive understanding of the Craft. Through open and respectful dialogue, Freemasons can gain new insights, challenge their preconceptions, and strengthen the bonds that unite them as brothers in pursuit of light and truth.

When you infuse every aspect of Lodge life with Masonic principles, even the most routine activities can be imbued with deeper meaning. A powerful way to set the tone for each gathering is to begin meetings with a brief contemplation on a specific Masonic symbol or teaching. This practice not only centers thoughts on the spiritual aspects of the Craft but also provides a thematic foundation for the evening's proceedings.

When addressing practical matters, such as financial reports or membership statistics, an effort should be made to relate these mundane details to broader Masonic principles. For instance, a discussion on the Lodge's finances could be framed within the context of stewardship and responsibility, while membership trends might be examined through the lens of brotherhood and community impact. By drawing these connections, even the most practical discussions can serve as opportunities for Masonic education and reflection.

Finally, to bookend the meeting with spiritual significance, Lodges should consider closing their gatherings with a moment of collective reflection. This brief period allows members to contemplate how the evening's work—whether it was ritual practice, business discussion, or fraternal bonding—contributes to their individual Masonic journeys. By implementing these practices,

Lodges can ensure that every meeting, regardless of its primary focus, reinforces the fundamental principles of Freemasonry and contributes to the spiritual growth of its members.

Ritual Integration

A beehive has its seasons and cycles. A Lodge, too, should establish a rhythm that balances inner and outer work. Healthy portions of both will lead to an idealized Masonic experience that benefits the Masons and the community.

To foster this balanced and vibrant Lodge experience, it is essential to create a structured approach that honors both the practical and speculative aspects of the Craft. One strategy is to designate certain meetings specifically for business matters, while reserving others entirely for education or degree work. In theory, this separation allows the Lodge to maintain its operational efficiency without sacrificing the deeper intellectual and spiritual engagement that is crucial to Masonry's mission. Business meetings can be focused, efficient, and goal-oriented, ensuring that the necessary administrative tasks are handled with clarity and purpose. In contrast, meetings dedicated to education or degree work can be immersive, providing a space for reflection, learning, and the performance of ritual in its most meaningful form. In practice, Lodges have varying levels of success maintaining a schedule of this nature.

In addition to restructuring regular meetings, the Lodge should consider planning an annual retreat devoted exclusively to Masonic philosophy and personal development. Such a retreat would offer members the opportunity to step away from the day-to-day concerns of Lodge management and immerse themselves in the deeper teachings of the Craft. A focused, multi-day retreat can foster a sense of brotherhood and shared purpose, creating a space for personal transformation and collective renewal. This time away would not only strengthen individual members' understanding of Masonic principles but could also reinvigorate the Lodge's commitment to its speculative work.

To ensure that these efforts are not fleeting but part of a consistent process of growth and self-assessment, a Lodge could implement quarterly "checkpoint" meetings. These gatherings would serve as moments to evaluate the Lodge's progress in both practical and speculative realms. Are the administrative functions running smoothly? Are members actively engaging in the educational opportunities provided? Are the core values of Masonry being reflected in the Lodge's activities? By regularly assessing these areas, the Lodge can stay aligned with its goals, making adjustments as needed to ensure ongoing improvement and harmony between its Operative and Speculative dimensions.

Masonic ritual stands as one of the most profound elements of the Craft, serving as the perfect synthesis of practical action and philosophical meaning. It is through ritual that Freemasons connect the Operative—the tangible, hands-on work of the Lodge—with the Speculative—the deeper exploration of moral and spiritual truths. By approaching ritual with intention and understanding, Lodges can unlock its full potential as a tool for personal and collective transformation.

To fully appreciate the ritual, it is essential to provide comprehensive education on the symbolism and allegory embedded within each degree. Every movement, word, and symbol in Masonic ritual carries a deeper meaning, and members should be encouraged to explore these layers of significance. Offering structured instruction on the origins and intentions behind the rituals will help Masons move beyond mere performance, allowing them to experience the ritual as a living embodiment of Masonic principles.

Officers, in particular, should be encouraged to deeply study and internalize the meaning of their roles within the ritual. Each officer's position is not just a function of governance but a symbolic representation of larger Masonic truths. W. Kirk MacNulty suggested that the officers of the Lodge could be thought of as a model of the psyche from a Jungian psychological perspective.[143] By committing to a deeper understanding of these roles, officers can bring greater intention and energy to their work, thereby elevating the overall experience for the Lodge.

To further enrich the Lodge's connection to ritual, special meetings—Lodges of Instruction—can be organized to explore a single aspect of ritual in depth. Rather than rushing through degree work, these focused sessions allow members to dissect and reflect on individual components of the ritual, such as a particular symbol, phrase, or movement. This approach cultivates a deeper connection to the Craft and helps demystify rituals for newer members, while offering seasoned Masons fresh insight into familiar practices.

Beyond its esoteric significance, ritual can also be framed as a tool for personal and collective growth. By treating ritual practice as a form of meditation or mindfulness exercise, Masons can develop a heightened sense of presence and focus during ceremonies. Each movement and recitation becomes an opportunity to center the mind, calm the body, and engage with the ritual's deeper teachings on a more profound level.

An important step in this process is discussing how the lessons of each degree can be applied to daily life. The moral and ethical teachings expressed through Masonic ritual are not meant to remain confined to the Lodge room; rather, they are guides for how members should conduct themselves in the world. Encouraging open dialogue about how Masonic principles—such as integrity, justice, and brotherly love—can be integrated into everyday actions will help bring the speculative work of the Lodge into practical reality.

By treating ritual as a bridge between the Operative and Spe-

---

143 W. Kirk MacNulty, *The Way of the Craftsman: Deluxe Edition* (Washington, D.C.: Plumbstone, 2017), 58–71.

culative aspects of Masonry, Lodges can ensure that even the most practical elements of Lodge work are imbued with deeper meaning. In restoring this balance between practical operations and speculative pursuit, we honor the full spectrum of Masonic tradition. Like the harmonious functioning of a beehive, where each action serves both immediate needs and higher purposes, a well-balanced Lodge creates an environment where administrative efficiency supports and enhances the pursuit of Masonic light. This integration ensures that every aspect of Lodge life, from the mundane to the profound, contributes to the transformative journey of each brother and the collective wisdom of the fraternity.

Change Management

Like a beehive adapting to environmental changes, Masonic Lodges must evolve to meet the challenges of the modern world while preserving their essential nature. Implementing the changes discussed herein requires careful planning, clear communication, and a commitment to continuous improvement.

We have already touched on ways to create a contemplative environment within the Lodge room. However, the communications themselves are also improved through practices that encourage mindfulness and reinforce the sacred nature of our work. Some Lodges have had success using small changes that can make big impacts such as:

- Begin each meeting with a short guided meditation or moment of silence
- Include time for personal reflection after degree ceremonies or significant Masonic teachings
- Encourage officers to share brief reflections on their roles and experiences

• Close meetings with a period of quiet contemplation on the lessons or work of the evening

Masonic Lodges can breathe new life into their administrative and operational tasks by aligning them with the rich symbolism and teachings of the fraternity. Rather than viewing these duties as mere chores, members should be encouraged to see them as integral to their individual Masonic journey and the collective mission of the Lodge.

For example, managing the Lodge's finances can be framed as an expression of the cardinal virtue of Temperance, or the Prudential stewardship over resources entrusted to the Craft. Organizing community service projects demonstrates the Masonic principle of relief, caring for the needs of others. Maintaining the Lodge building and property upholds the value of industry, mirroring the tireless work ethic of the bees in the beehive.

Masonic symbols can also be incorporated into the operational contexts of the Lodge. The square and compass, for instance, can be used to explain the organizational structure and decision-making processes. The working tools can be related to the practical tasks required to keep the Lodge functioning effectively. And the beehive can serve as a powerful metaphor for the collaborative effort needed to address the administrative needs of the fraternity.

Furthermore, the Lodge's community engagement efforts should be framed within the broader Masonic teachings. Charitable works can be emphasized as embodying the virtue of brotherly love, extending care and support to those beyond the membership. Volunteer activities can be connected to the principle of relief, highlighting how Masons fulfill their duty to aid those in distress. And the Lodge's public presence and outreach can be discussed as contributing to the Masonic mission of making good men better and the world a better place.

By consistently relating the practical aspects of Lodge life to

Masonic principles, symbol study, and the larger purpose of the fraternity, the Lodge can help members view their responsibilities not merely as chores, but as opportunities to apply and deepen their Masonic knowledge and virtues. This approach fosters a culture where every member understands how their participation, whether in administrative tasks, community service, or other operational duties, is integral to their personal Masonic development and the collective journey of the Lodge.

The true strength of a beehive lies not just in its efficient operation, but in the perfect balance it maintains between practical labor and the higher purpose of sustaining the colony. Similarly, a Masonic Lodge must strive to harmonize its operational necessities with its speculative and philosophical aims.

Before engaging upon any significant undertaking, it's crucial to understand the current state of your Lodge. The Lodge is likely stronger than you expect in some areas, and more deficient in some areas than you might have hoped. To gain a comprehensive understanding of your Lodge's current state, consider implementing the following suggestions.

ANALYZE ATTENDANCE PATTERNS AND ENGAGEMENT LEVELS IN VARIOUS LODGE ACTIVITIES

Begin by reviewing attendance records for regular meetings, special events, and educational programs over the past year or two. Look for trends in participation—are certain types of events more popular? Are there specific times of year when attendance dips? Additionally, assess the level of engagement during these activities. Are members actively participating in discussions, volunteering for tasks, or simply attending passively (if they attend at all?)

REVIEW FINANCIAL RECORDS TO UNDERSTAND RESOURCE ALLOCATION AND EFFICIENCY

Conduct a thorough examination of the Lodge's financial statements, including income sources, expenditures, and reserves. Pay close attention to how resources are allocated across different areas such as building maintenance, charitable activities, education programs, and social events. This analysis can reveal whether the Lodge's spending aligns with its stated priorities and values.

ASSESS THE BALANCE BETWEEN OPERATIONAL TASKS AND SPECULATIVE PURSUITS

Evaluate how much time and energy is devoted to administrative tasks versus Masonic education and philosophical discussions. Are business meetings dominating the Lodge's agenda at the expense of more profound Masonic work? Consider surveying members to gauge their satisfaction with this balance and their desires for change.

COMPARE YOUR LODGE'S PRACTICES WITH THE IDEALS OUTLINED IN MASONIC TEACHINGS

Review key Masonic texts and teachings, such as Anderson's *Constitutions* or the *Ahiman Rezon*, and assess how well your Lodge's current practices align with these ideals. Are there areas where the Lodge has drifted from its core principles or neglected important aspects of Masonic tradition?

LOOK FOR DISCREPANCIES BETWEEN STATED GOALS AND ACTUAL OUTCOMES

Examine the Lodge's mission statement or annual goals (if they exist) and compare them to actual achievements. Are there recurring goals that never seem to be met? Are there successes that aren't being adequately recognized or built upon? This comparison can highlight areas where the Lodge may need to refocus its efforts or adjust its expectations.

IDENTIFY BOTTLENECKS OR INEFFICIENCIES IN LODGE OPERATIONS

Analyze the Lodge's operational processes, from how meetings are conducted to how new members are introduced to the Craft. Look for areas where tasks are duplicated, communication breaks down, or resources are underutilized. Pay particular attention to any recurring complaints or frustrations expressed by members, as these often point to operational inefficiencies.

By employing these assessments, Lodges can gain a clear and objective understanding of their current state. This self-awareness is crucial for developing targeted strategies for improvement and renewal. Just as bees continually assess and adjust their hive to ensure its health and productivity, Masonic Lodges must engage in regular self-examination to maintain their vitality and relevance.

Remember, the goal is not to criticize or assign blame, but to identify areas of strength to build upon and areas of weakness to address. With this knowledge in hand, Lodges can begin to chart a course for meaningful change and growth, always guided by the timeless principles of Freemasonry.

COMMUNICATE OPENLY AND FREQUENTLY
ABOUT THE REASONS FOR AND BENEFITS
OF PROPOSED CHANGES

Transparency is key. Regular updates through various channels (meetings, emails, newsletters) can keep members informed and engaged. Clear communication can prevent misunderstandings and rumors that often derail change efforts. Involve a variety of perspectives, if possible including long-time members and newer initiates, officers and regular members. This diversity can bring valuable insights and help address concerns from different segments of the Lodge membership.

By proactively addressing resistance and building consensus, Lodges can navigate the challenges of change more smoothly. Remember, when we put love in action, it "extends beyond the grave, through the boundless realms of eternity."[144] This perspective can help frame changes not as threats to tradition, but as necessary steps to ensure Freemasonry's continued relevance and positive impact.

With a clear understanding of the Lodge's current state, the next step is to develop a structured plan for improvement. This process mirrors the organized and purposeful nature of a beehive, where each bee has a role in contributing to the colony's overall success.

The key to effective change is setting goals that are both ambitious and attainable. We set our aims high, while remaining grounded in practical reality. Rev. Tapley reminds Masons that "In the first Place; let Us always consider, That when we enter the Lodge, we are in a Place, where Masons meet to work: That Wisdom, Strength, and Beauty, are its chief Supports."[145]

144 Jeremy Ladd Cross, *The True Masonic Chart, or Hieroglyphic Monitor; Containing All the Emblems Explained in the Degrees...* (New Haven, Conn.: T. Woodward, 1826), 16.

145 Rev. Tapley, A *Charge Delivered to the Brethren of the Most Ancient and Honourable Society of Free and Accepted Masons* (London, 1751), 4.

Evaluate your available information to identify which areas, if improved, would have the most significant positive impact on the Lodge. Consider both the potential benefits and the resources required for each improvement. For instance, enhancing the quality of ritual work might have a profound effect on member engagement and requires primarily time and effort, making it a high-priority, high-feasibility goal.

SET SMART GOALS (SPECIFIC, MEASURABLE, ACHIEVABLE, RELEVANT, TIME-BOUND)

SMART goals are something that create a strong aversion in some people. Regardless of how corporate culture has ruined the term, this acronym for creating goals does provide a clear framework for action and accountability. For example, instead of a vague goal like "improve Masonic education," a SMART goal might be: "Implement a monthly Masonic education program, with 30-minute presentations on different aspects of Masonic history and philosophy, to be delivered by a rotation of volunteer members, starting in the next quarter."

Every goal should serve the dual purpose of improving Lodge operations and advancing Masonic values. Therefore, even operational goals should be framed within the context of Masonic teachings and principles. William Smith advises Masons to "With all Expedition, pursue the Knowledge of the Craft, and endeavour to become perfect therein."[146]

Effective implementation requires clear structure and accountability. This approach echoes the organized labor division within a beehive, where each bee has specific tasks contributing to the hive's overall function. One way to accomplish this is to break down large goals into manageable tasks or milestones.

146 Smith, *The Book M, Or, Masonry Triumphant*, 1:18.

Complex goals should be divided into smaller, achievable steps. For instance, if the goal is to revamp the Lodge's mentoring program, milestones might include researching successful mentoring programs in other Lodges, drafting a new mentoring curriculum, training mentors, and piloting the program with new initiates.

Specific responsibilities can be assigned to officers, committees, or individual members. Clear ownership is crucial for progress. Responsibilities should be assigned based on members' skills, interests, and capacity. This not only ensures tasks are completed but also fosters a sense of personal investment in the Lodge's improvement.

To maintain accountability, establish clear deadlines for each phase of implementation. Deadlines create a sense of urgency and help maintain momentum. They should be realistic but firm, taking into account the Lodge's calendar and members' other commitments.

By developing a structured action plan with clear goals, responsibilities, and timelines, Lodges can transform their aspirations for improvement into tangible progress. This methodical approach, reminiscent of the orderly workings of a beehive, ensures that every member has a role in the Lodge's renewal and that efforts are coordinated towards common objectives.

Remember, the temple is not yet completed. The goal is not perfection, but steady, meaningful improvement. As the Lodge works through its action plan, it should remain flexible and open to adjusting its approach based on new insights and changing circumstances. This adaptability, combined with a clear vision and structured plan, will help ensure the Lodge's continued vitality and relevance in the face of modern challenges.

Change, even when necessary and beneficial, often faces resistance. This is as true in Masonic Lodges as it is in beehives when adapting to new environmental conditions. Addressing this resistance proactively is crucial for the successful implementation of any improvement plan.

Anticipating and preparing for potential objections is a key step in managing resistance to change. Common objections in Masonic Lodges often stem from a desire to preserve tradition and maintain the familiar. The problem is, they often do not understand exactly what it is they are preserving.

Be prepared to hear phrases like:

- We've always done it this way
- This isn't customary
- In my year....

These objections often mask deeper fears about losing the essence of Freemasonry or diluting its values. They speak to the desire of all Good Masons to see "its sacred mysteries are safely lodged in the repository of faithful breasts."[147] They are particularly attentive to make sure there is "no alteration or innovation in the body of Masonry."[148] To this aim, ensure that all new endeavors are firmly established in Masonic practice.

When addressing objections, always tie your arguments back to core Masonic values and the overall goal of Lodge improvement. For instance, if proposing to modernize communication methods, emphasize how this aligns with the Masonic principle of brotherly love by fostering better connection among members.

Freemasonry has withstood many eras of evolution and adaptation. A common Lodge fixture, the "three lesser lights" were described as "three burning tapers, or candles placed on candlesticks (some say or candles on pedestals)."[149] And yet, in many contemporary Lodges, these are provided via some form of electric light.

147 Preston, *Illustrations of Masonry: A Grand Gala in Honour of Free Masonry, Held at the Crown and Anchor Tavern, in the Strand* (1772), 14.

148 William Preston, *Illustrations of Masonry*, 2nd ed. (London: Printed for J. Wilkie, No. 71. St. Paul's Church Yard, 1775), 120.

149 Morgan, *Illustrations of Masonry, by One of the Fraternity, Who Has Devoted Thirty Years to the Subject*, 20.

Nothing can substitute for live flame, but many Lodge buildings have insurance requirements preventing the use of fire. Highlighting such historical adaptations can demonstrate that change, when thoughtfully implemented, has been crucial to Freemasonry's longevity.

Focus on the positive outcomes of proposed changes. For example, if suggesting more emphasis on Masonic education, highlight how this can deepen members' understanding and appreciation of the Craft, potentially leading to greater engagement and satisfaction. You'll find that when the Lodge starts to create exalted experiences, more men will want to take part in the Craft.

Building consensus is crucial for successful implementation of changes. This process should mirror the collaborative nature of a beehive, where the collective good is paramount. All work is for naught if the Fraternity fails to produce true Masons. The Lodge, to the extent possible, should be "all of one mind."[150] Thaddeus Mason Harris invoked Isaiah 49:9 when he said, "Let it not be supposed that you have here 'LABOURED in vain, and spent your STRENGTH for nought.'"[151]

Like a well-functioning hive, a harmonious Masonic Lodge operates with efficiency and purpose, where every action contributes to the greater good of the fraternity and its members.

Streamlining administrative tasks, focusing on core Masonic values, and balancing practical operations with speculative pursuits can revitalize our Lodges. By implementing these strategies, we create an environment where the mundane aspects of running an organization support and enhance the profound work of personal and collective transformation that is at the heart of Freemasonry.

Remember that the goal of operational excellence is not efficiency for its own sake, but rather to create space and energy for the

150   Harris, *Constitutions of the Ancient and Honourable Fraternity of Free and Accepted Masons*, 175.

151   Harris, 175.

deeper work of Masonry. When we reduce distractions and focus our efforts, we allow the light of Masonic wisdom to shine more brightly in our Lodges and in our lives.

As you work to implement these ideas in your own Lodge, approach the task with the same dedication, patience, and collective spirit that bees bring to their hive. Each small improvement, each thoughtful change, contributes to the overall harmony and vitality of your Masonic home.

Let us strive to create Lodges where, like the ceaseless hum of a thriving beehive, there is a constant, harmonious blend of practical labor and spiritual pursuit. In doing so, we honor the rich tradition of our Craft while ensuring its relevance and power for future generations of seekers. May your Lodges be filled with the sweet honey of wisdom, the industrious spirit of true brotherhood, and the transformative power of Masonic light.

9

Healing the Craft through Harmony

THE BEEHIVE has long served as a powerful symbol in Freemasonry, representing industry, cooperation, and collective
wisdom. This metaphor extends beyond mere physical labor to encompass the spiritual and intellectual work of the Craft.
In the context of harmony, the beehive offers a compelling model
of how individual efforts, when properly coordinated, can create a
thriving and harmonious whole.

In a well-functioning hive, each bee has its role, working in
concert with its fellows to ensure the colony's survival and prosperity. This intricate balance of individual effort and collective purpose
mirrors the ideal state of a Masonic Lodge, where brothers work
together in harmony to achieve the goals of the Craft.

Harmony has been a cornerstone of Masonic thought since the earliest days of Speculative Freemasonry. *The Constitutions of the Free-Masons*, published by James Anderson in 1723, emphasizes the importance of harmony in its charges, cautioning that unbecoming behavior would "blast our Harmony, and defeat our laudable Purposes."[152] Anderson continues:

> Therefore no private Piques or Quarrels must be brought within the Door of the Lodge, far less any Quarrels about Religion, or Nations, or State Policy, we being only, as Masons, of the [Religion in which all Men agree] we are also of all Nations, Tongues, Kindreds, and Languages, and are resolved against all Politics, as what never yet conducted to the Welfare of the Lodge, nor ever will. This Charge has been always strictly enjoined and observed.[153]

This sentiment has been echoed in Preston's work also where he charges, "These laws are to be strictly observed, that harmony may be preserved, and the business of the Lodge be carried on with order and regularity."[154]

This emphasis on harmony is not merely for the sake of peaceful coexistence, but is fundamental to the transformative work of Freemasonry. Just as a beehive cannot function effectively amidst chaos and discord, a Masonic Lodge cannot fulfill its purpose of making good men better if it is plagued by disharmony.

The concept of harmony in Freemasonry goes beyond mere absence of conflict. It encompasses the idea of working together in

152 James Anderson, *The Constitutions of the Free-Masons: Containing the History, Charges, Regulations, &c. of That Most Ancient and Right Worshipful Fraternity. For the Use of the Lodges* (London: printed by William Hunter, for John Senex, and John Hooke, 1723), 54.

153 Ibid.

154 Preston, *Illustrations of Masonry: A Grand Gala in Honour of Free Masonry, Held at the Crown and Anchor Tavern, in the Strand*, 6.

concord towards shared goals, each brother contributing his unique talents and perspectives to create something greater than the sum of its parts. This ideal of harmony reflects the broader principles that influenced early Speculative Freemasonry, particularly the notion of societal progress through cooperation and shared knowledge.

The beehive model of harmony can guide us in addressing the challenges facing modern Freemasonry, offering practical strategies for fostering unity and concord within our Lodges.

Understanding Discord

Even the most well-organized hives can face disruptions. Similarly, our Lodges, despite their focus on harmony and brotherly love, are not immune to discord. To truly heal our Craft, we must first understand the nature of the conflicts that arise within our halls.

In many Lodges across the world, a generational divide has begun to emerge. As we strive to attract younger members to ensure the future of our Craft, we sometimes find ourselves at odds with the very traditions we seek to preserve. The young initiate, eager for enlightenment and meaningful ritual, may clash with the seasoned Past Master who views any change as a threat to the Landmarks of the Order. This tension, like a discordant note in the harmony of the hive, can disrupt the smooth functioning of the Lodge.

Ritual, the very cornerstone of our Craft, can paradoxically become a source of conflict. As any experienced Mason knows, variations in ritual performance exist not just between jurisdictions, but often between Lodges in the same town. Atmospheric or aesthetic differences one brother considers to be vital elements of the ceremony, another may view as unnecessary flourish. These disagreements, though often rooted in a shared love for the Craft, can create rifts that undermine the unity we strive to achieve.

The management of Lodge resources, both financial and human, can also breed discord. In these trying economic times, debates over dues, charitable contributions, and the allocation of funds can become heated. Some brothers may push for increased spending on community outreach, while others advocate for conserving resources. These financial quandaries, much like a shortage of nectar in the hive, can strain relationships and test the bonds of brotherhood.

Leadership conflicts, too, can disrupt the harmony of the Lodge. The yearly change of officers, while designed to give all worthy brothers a chance to serve, can sometimes lead to power struggles or disagreements about the direction of the Lodge. A Worshipful Master with grand plans for change may face resistance from those comfortable with the status quo, creating tension that ripples through the entire membership.

Lastly, we must acknowledge that Masons, for all our aspirations to virtue, are still human. Personality clashes, misunderstandings, and simple differences of opinion can create interpersonal conflicts that, if left unaddressed, can poison the atmosphere of the Lodge.

The impact of such discord can be profound and far-reaching. Like a disease in the hive, disharmony in the Lodge can lead to decreased attendance, as brothers seek to avoid conflict rather than confront it. The transformative work of Freemasonry is severely hindered when energy is diverted to managing conflicts rather than pursuing enlightenment.

Moreover, internal strife can sometimes spill over into the public sphere, tarnishing the reputation of Freemasonry in the broader community. A Lodge known for its discord will struggle to attract new members, as potential initiates sense the tension and disunity beyond the Tyler's door.

In nature, when a hive faces threats or disruptions, the bees do not abandon their work. Instead, they redouble their efforts, working in concert to address the issue and restore balance. So too must we, as Masons, face our conflicts head-on, armed with the principles of brotherly love, relief, and truth that form the foundation of our Craft.

Brotherly love is of paramount importance. According to our original book of *Constitutions*, it is both the "Foundation and Cape-Stone, the Cement and Glory of this ancient Fraternity."[155] This metaphor continues in Webb, where "the cement of brotherly love, and affection... unites us into one sacred band, or society of friends and brothers, among whom no contention should ever exist, but that noble contention or rather emulation, of who best can work, or best agree."[156]

The authors were giving an important illustration. In order for the rough stones to fit together nicely, mortar cement is used. As Webb said, "nothing can be united without proper cement."[157] Sometimes it is used copiously. Freemasons, also, must liberally apply this cement if they are to continue to build the House not made with hands.[158]

Harmony through Resolution

One of the most crucial skills in maintaining harmony is active listening. This involves not just hearing the words spoken by our brothers, but truly seeking to understand their perspective. In the spirit of the beehive, where each bee's contribution is vital, we must value and consider every voice of the active workers of our Lodge.

Freemasonry teaches us to seek Truth as "a divine attribute"

155 Anderson, *The Constitutions of the Free-Masons* (1723), 56.
156 Thomas Smith Webb, *The Freemason's Monitor; or, Illustrations of Masonry: In Two Parts* (New York: Printed by Southwick and Crooker No. 354, Water-Street, 1802), 74.
157 Thomas Smith Webb, *The Freemason's Monitor; or, Illustrations of Masonry: In Two Parts* (Albany: Printed for Spencer and Webb, Market-Street, 1797), 117.
158 2 Corinthians 5:1.

and "the foundation of all Masonic virtues."[159] In our interactions with our brothers, we must strive for open and honest dialogue. This means creating an environment where all members feel safe expressing their thoughts and concerns without fear of ridicule or retribution.

Just as a beehive thrives on the diverse roles of its inhabitants, our Lodges should celebrate the diversity of our membership. This includes not just demographic diversity, but also diversity of thought and experience.

Empathy is a cornerstone of Masonic teachings. Preston writes that "To sooth[e] the unhappy, to sympathize with their misfortunes, to compassionate their miseries, and to restore peace to their troubled minds, is the grand aim we have in view."[160] By putting ourselves in our brothers shoes, we can better understand their actions and motivations, fostering a more harmonious Lodge environment.

Lodge leaders must embody the principles of harmony they wish to see in their Lodge. This means demonstrating respect, practicing active listening, and addressing conflicts promptly and fairly.

When conflicts do arise, Lodge leaders should be prepared to mediate. This involves remaining impartial, hearing all sides, and working towards solutions that benefit the Lodge as a whole.

Harmony through Music

Music has long played a crucial role in Masonic ritual and gatherings. From the earliest days of Speculative Freemasonry, songs and

159 Thomas Dunckerley, *The Light and Truth of Masonry Explained, Being the Substance of a Charge Delivered at Plymouth, in April, 1757, by Thomas Dunckerley, Esq., P.G.M* (London: Davey & Law, 1757), 6.

160 William Preston, *Illustrations of Masonry*, 2nd ed. (London: Printed for J. Wilkie, No. 71. St. Paul's Church Yard, 1775), 72.

hymns have been used to reinforce Masonic teachings and create a sense of unity among brothers and fellows.

In Freemasonry, music served a dual purpose:

- It was a vehicle for understanding deeper metaphysical concepts of proportion and harmony, extending beyond mere aesthetic pleasure.
- It was a participatory activity in which all Masons were expected to engage, rather than a performance art.[161]

The practice of collective music-making, particularly during post-Lodge feasts, was an integral part of Masonic culture. This communal musical tradition wasn't just entertainment, but a core element of Masonic practice and brotherhood.[162]

Masonic songs often contain profound messages about brotherly love, moral virtue, and the quest for enlightenment. As Malcolm Davies said, "these songs can be seen as an expression of Masonic thought."[163] Davies also wrote that Masonic songs "more perhaps than any other Masonic source, demonstrate the development of the ideals of Freemasonry."[164] By revisiting and understanding these songs, we can reinforce the core values that bind us as Masons.

The act of singing together creates a powerful sense of unity. Whether it's opening odes, closing hymns, or songs during the Fes-

161 Nathan A. St. Pierre, "'Genius of Masonry': The Preservation of Masonic Tradition in the Songs of the Freemasons," in *Exploring Early Grand Lodge Freemasonry: Studies in Honor of the Tricentennial of the Establishment of the Grand Lodge of England*, ed. Christopher B. Murphy and Shawn Eyer (Washington, D.C.: Plumbstone, 2017), 281.

162 Katherine Campbell, "Masonic Song in Scotland: Folk Tunes and Community," *Oral Tradition* 27, no. 1 (2012): 88.

163 Malcolm Davies, *The Masonic Muse: Songs, Music and Musicians Associated with Dutch Freemasonry, 1730–1806* (Koninklijke Vereniging voor Nederlandse Muziekgeschiedenis, 2005), 33.

164 Davies, *The Masonic Muse*, 238–39.

tive Board, group singing can help brothers feel more connected to each other and to the Craft.

Group singing has been shown to have powerful social bonding effects. Singing together can create a strong sense of belonging and encourage greater community involvement. The social bonding effect of group singing appears to be a stable characteristic, persisting even in the face of environmental and situational influences.[165]

Some Masonic rituals incorporate musical elements. These shared experiences, repeated over time, can create deep bonds between brothers and reinforce the lessons of Freemasonry. Always look for every opportunity to add music to the Lodge experience. The *Ahimon Rezon* commands us to "hinder not music."[166]

Lodges could consider incorporating discussions of Masonic music into their educational programs. This could include exploring the history and meaning of traditional Masonic songs, or even learning to perform them together. At the very least, Matthew Birkhead's *Enter'd Prentice's Song* is truly a lasting and meaningful Masonic experience that will elevate any first degree (see Fig. 3).

Integration Strategies

Harmony is essential to the health and vitality of our Lodges. Like a well-functioning beehive, a harmonious Lodge is one where each member contributes their unique talents towards a common goal. There are sources of discord that can disrupt this harmony, from

165 David A. Camlin, Helena Daffern, and Katherine Zeserson, "Group Singing as a Resource for the Development of a Healthy Public: A Study of Adult Group Singing," *Humanities and Social Sciences Communications* 7, no. 1 (August 5, 2020): 1–15.

166 Laurence Dermott, *Ahiman Rezon: Or, A Help to a Brother; Shewing the Excellency of Secrecy, and the First Cause, or Motive, of the Institution of Free-Masonry [&c. Followed by] A Choice Collection of Masons Songs* (London: James Bedford, 1756), xv.

generational differences to resource management issues, but we have strategies for restoring balance when conflicts arise.

The pursuit of harmony in our Lodges is not a destination, but an ongoing journey. Just as the bees in a hive must constantly work to maintain their colony's balance, we as Masons must continually strive to foster harmony in our Lodges. This requires vigilance, open communication, and a commitment to our shared Masonic values.

Every Mason has a role to play in creating and maintaining harmony within their Lodge. Whether it's practicing active listening, participating in Lodge music, or simply treating each brother with respect and kindness, each small action contributes to the overall harmony of the Lodge. Let us each commit to being like the industrious bee, working tirelessly for the good of the hive.

After all, it has been said that "harmony" is part of what "gives strength and stability to the whole."[167] By committing to harmony in our Lodges, we not only enhance our own Masonic experience but also strengthen the foundation of our beloved Craft for generations to come.

As we continue to steward Grand Lodge-era Freemasonry, the beehive emerges not merely as a relic of our past, but as a living symbol—a guide for our present and a beacon for our future. Throughout this exploration, we have repeatedly demonstrated the multifaceted significance of the beehive, uncovering layers of meaning that speak directly to the challenges and opportunities facing our Craft today.

---

167 Dyer, *William Preston and His Work*, 197.

The Enter'd 'Prentice's Song
THE FREE MASON'S HEALTH

Words and Music by Matthew Birkhead (d. 1722)

Fig. 3. The Free-Mason's Health, or the Enter'd Prentice's Song, first published in 1709.

3. 'Tis This, and 'tis That,
   They cannot tell What,
   Why so many Great Men of the Nation
   Should Aprons put on,
   To make themselves one
   With a Free and an Accepted Mason.

4. Great Kings, Dukes, and Lords,
   Have laid by their Swords,
   Our Myst'ry to put a good Grace on,
   And ne'er been asham'd
   To hear themselves nam'd
   With a Free and an Accepted Mason.

5. Antiquity's Pride
   We have on our side,
   And it maketh Men just in their Station:
   There's nought but what's good
   To be understood
   By a Free and an Accepted Mason.

6. Then join Hand in Hand,
   T'each other firm stand,
   Let's be merry, and put a bright Face on:
   What Mortal can boast
   So NOBLE A TOAST,
   As a Free and an Accepted Mason?

The Hive Recapitulated:
Lessons in Masonic Life

Industry, Cooperation, and Balance

T HE BEEHIVE, first and foremost, stands as a testament to
the virtue of industry. From the earliest days of Speculative Masonry, this symbol has urged us toward diligent
labor, both in the Operative sense of our daily vocations and in
the speculative realm of self-improvement. So much so, that to re-
fuse to engage in this pursuit risked violent expulsion. As we have
seen, the decline of Freemasonry in recent decades can be partly
attributed to a waning of this industrial spirit—a complacency that
has allowed our Lodges to become mere social clubs rather than
workshops for the soul.

Yet, the beehive reminds us that true Masonic labor is never
done. Like the ceaseless activity of bees, our work in perfecting ourselves and our Craft must be constant and purposeful. This industry
extends beyond the confines of the Lodge room, challenging us to
apply Masonic principles in every aspect of our lives. The ways of
Virtue are indeed beautiful.[168]

Perhaps no lesson from the beehive is more crucial to Free-

168 Proverbs 3:17.

masonry's future than that of cooperation. In a well-functioning hive, each bee plays its part, contributing to the collective good. So too must our Lodges function as harmonious units, with every brother offering his unique talents and perspectives to strengthen the whole.

Discord—whether arising from generational divides, ritual variations, or simple personality clashes—can undermine the fabric of our fraternity. Masonic tradition holds that among the Ancient Brethren "discord was unknown, still silence reigned, and to disturb the general quiet, even the sound of metal was unheard."[169] Preston posits:

> Is it not then evident that Masonry is an universal advantage to mankind? Unless discord and harmony be the same, it must be so. It is likewise reconcilable to the best policy, as it prevents that heat of passion and those partial animosities which different interests too often create.[170]

The beehive helps promote this harmony by showing us that diversity, when properly harnessed, becomes a source of strength rather than division. By fostering open communication, mutual respect, and a shared sense of purpose, we can create Lodges that truly embody the Masonic ideal of unity.

The beehive offers modern Freemasonry the importance of balance. Just as a hive must balance the practical tasks of gathering nectar and building comb with the higher purpose of sustaining the colony, our Lodges must find equilibrium between their Operative (the hive itself) and Speculative (the honey) functions.

Many Lodges have tilted too far toward the Operative—becoming consumed with administrative tasks, financial concerns, and

169 Dyer, *William Preston and His Work*, 238.

170 William Preston, *Illustrations of Masonry*, 2nd ed. (London: Printed for J. Wilkie, No. 71. St. Paul's Church Yard, 1775), 17.

the mechanics of degree work. Others have swung to the opposite extreme, neglecting the practical realities of running a Lodge in pursuit of esoteric knowledge. The beehive teaches us that both aspects are essential and must be harmonized for the Craft to thrive in the twenty-first century.

We are called to be both workers and philosophers, craftsmen and seekers. By embracing both the practical and the speculative aspects of Masonry, we can achieve a fuller, richer experience of the Craft, one that transforms not only ourselves but the world around us.

Excellence in Lodge Practice

While Masons broadly agree on the importance of quality in lodge work, there are varying perspectives on how best to achieve and maintain high standards. Contemporary Masonic authors have approached this question from different angles. Some advocate for a particularly rigorous approach emphasizing formal dress, precise ritual, and careful attention to traditional Masonic customs via decorum. For example, Andrew Hammer in *Observing the Craft* states "Freemasonry was never intended, and cannot be allowed, to make good men ordinary."[171] Others, like Shawn Eyer, propose a more nuanced framework based on three key principles: SPECULATIVE PURPOSE, INITIATIC EMPHASIS, and TRADITIONAL BASIS.[172]

---

171 Andrew Hammer, *Observing the Craft: The Pursuit of Excellence in Masonic Labour and Observance*, First Edition (Alexandria, Va.: Mindhive Books, 2010), 80.

172 Shawn Eyer, "A Classical Vision of Masonic Restoration," *Philalethes: The Journal of Masonic Research and Letters* 66, no. 4 (2013): 149. This article recommends that lodge activities fit at least one, and preferably all three, of the principles in order to stay consistent with the historical purposes of Craft Freemasonry.

The beehive teaches us that excellence emerges from the harmonious integration of multiple approaches. Just as each bee contributes its unique talents within established patterns of behavior, Lodges must find their own authentic path to quality while remaining true to fundamental Masonic principles. This requires each Lodge to give thoughtful consideration to various elements that Eyer describes as the "practical tradition"—the embodied practices and ancient usages that were "intentionally transmitted for the express purpose of sustaining a Masonic culture that would be consistent with the values, teachings, and purposes of the Craft."[173]

The key considerations include:

- The level of desired formality in dress and deportment
- The standards for ritual performance
- The balance between education and fellowship
- The pace and depth of candidate preparation
- The preservation of Lodge customs and Masonic Traditions

I do not advocate dogmatic adherence to any single model, but rather the sincere commitment to creating an environment where Masonic labor can flourish. The beehive shows us that high standards need not mean inflexibility. Rather, these standards provide the stable framework within which creativity and adaptation can occur. By maintaining appropriate standards while allowing for organic development, Lodges can remain both excellent and relevant as they guide us toward a future made bright by the Light we seek.

From Metaphor to Action

The beehive is more than a quaint symbol or a historical curiosity—it is a blueprint for Masonic renewal. As we look to the future

173   Eyer, "A Classical Vision of Masonic Restoration," 157.

of our fraternity, let us consider how we might apply these lessons in practical terms, rebuilding our Lodges into vibrant centers of Masonic Light.

First and foremost, we must rekindle the spirit of industry within our Lodges. This means moving beyond passive attendance to active participation. Every brother should be encouraged to contribute meaningfully to the life of the Lodge, whether through ritual work, educational presentations, or community service. There is no shortage of work to be done.

Moreover, we must extend this culture of engagement beyond the Lodge room. Freemasonry is not a ring to be donned and removed at will, but a way of life. Let us challenge ourselves and our brothers to apply Masonic principles in our daily lives, becoming living exemplars of the Craft in our families, workplaces, and communities.

To create truly cooperative Lodges, we need to bridge dissident views. Mentorship programs can bridge generational gaps, pairing experienced Masons with newer members to facilitate the transmission of knowledge and traditions. Regular brotherhood events, both within and outside the Lodge, can foster the personal connections that form the basis of true Masonic harmony.

Communication is key to this process. Open forums for discussion of Lodge matters can ensure that every voice is heard. By creating an environment where all brothers feel valued and included, we lay the groundwork for a more vibrant and resilient fraternity.

Achieving balance between the Operative and Speculative aspects of Masonry requires thoughtful planning and execution. Lodge meetings should be structured to include both necessary business and opportunities for intellectual and spiritual growth. This might involve alternating between administrative meetings and educational sessions, or incorporating philosophical discussions into every gathering.

Lodges must also strive to make their Operative work more meaningful by connecting it to Masonic principles and teachings.

Financial reports can be framed in terms of stewardship and responsibility. Charitable activities can be linked to the Masonic virtues of brotherly love and relief. By infusing our practical work with deeper meaning, we can ensure that even the most mundane tasks contribute to our speculative journey.

Central to rebuilding the Craft is a renewed commitment to Masonic education. The beehive has shown us the importance of producing "honey"—the sweet wisdom that results from dedicated study and reflection. Lodges should implement robust educational programs that go beyond rote memorization to explore the rich philosophical and historical dimensions of Freemasonry.

This educational renaissance should embrace both traditional and novel approaches. Lecture series, study groups, and guided readings can provide a solid foundation in Masonic knowledge. At the same time, interactive workshops, online resources, and multimedia presentations can also be engaging. The goal should be to create a culture of continuous learning, where every Mason is both student and teacher in the pursuit of Light.

The beehive has long been associated with the more esoteric aspects of Masonic tradition. In our efforts to revitalize the Craft, we must not shy away from these deeper currents of meaning. While maintaining the essential landmarks of Freemasonry, Lodges should provide opportunities for brothers to explore the esoteric and mystical dimensions of our symbolism and rituals.

This might involve forming special interest groups within the Lodge dedicated to studying topics like sacred geometry, Hermetic philosophy, or comparative religion. It could also mean incorporating meditative practices or symbolic exercises into Lodge activities. By reconnecting with our esoteric roots, we can offer a more profound and transformative Masonic experience, one that speaks to the spiritual hunger of our times.

A Call to Work

As we apply these lessons from the beehive, a vision of Freemasonry's future begins to emerge—one as bright and promising as the Craft's illustrious past. Imagine Lodges buzzing with activity, where brothers eagerly gather not out of mere habit or obligation, but drawn by the promise of genuine fellowship and intellectual stimulation. Picture ritual work performed with such depth of understanding and sincerity that it truly transforms both candidate and observer. Envision a fraternity so vibrant and relevant that men of quality seek it out, recognizing in Freemasonry a path to personal growth and societal improvement.

This imagined future requires dedication and effort from every Mason. Like the bees in their hive, we must each play our part in building and sustaining this vision. Whether we serve as officers, participate in degree work, contribute to educational programs, or simply attend meetings with enthusiasm and an open heart, every action adds to the collective strength of our Masonic hive.

Moreover, we must be willing to adapt and evolve while remaining true to our core principles. The beehive, for all its ancient symbolism, is a dynamic, living system. So too must Freemasonry be willing to embrace new ideas and methods while preserving the essential wisdom that has sustained it for centuries. This might mean leveraging technology to enhance our communications and educational efforts, or finding new ways to make Masonry relevant to younger generations without compromising its fundamental values.

The beehive stands as a constant reminder of these values. It challenges us to be ever-industrious in our Masonic labors, cooperative in our relations with our brothers, and balanced in our approach to the Craft. It urges us to produce the sweet honey of wisdom through diligent study and reflection, and to work harmoniously for the good of the entire Masonic community.

Let us, then, take up this charge with renewed vigor. Let every

Lodge become a thriving hive of Masonic activity, every brother an industrious worker in the great task of self-improvement and societal betterment. Let us build upon the foundation laid by our predecessors, creating a fraternity that is at once true to its ancient principles and vitally relevant to the modern world.

The future of Freemasonry lies in our hands. Like the bees returning to their hive laden with nectar, let us bring to our Lodges the fruits of our labor, the wisdom of our reflections, and the warmth of our brotherly love. In doing so, we ensure that the Light of Freemasonry continues to shine brightly, illuminating the path for generations of seekers to come. And so we pray:

May
the Great Architect
of the Universe guide and prosper
our efforts, as we labor to build and
maintain this noble hive of Freemasonry.
Hence all may see the benign influence
of Masonry, as all true Masons have done
from the beginning of the World, and will
do to the end of time. Amen. So Mote It Bee.[174]

174 Adapted from Preston, *Illustrations of Masonry* (1772), 48.

Bibliography

Adamson, Henry. *The Muses Threnodie, or, Mirthfull Mournings, on the Death of Master Gall Containing Varietie of Pleasant Poëticall Descriptions, Morall Instructions, Historicall Narrations, and Divine Observations, with the Most Remarkable Antiquities of Scotland, Especially at Perth By Mr. H. Adamson.* Printed at Edinburgh: In King James College, by George Anderson, 1638.

Anderson, James. *The Constitutions of the Free-Masons: Containing the History, Charges, Regulations, &c. of That Most Ancient and Right Worshipful Fraternity. For the Use of the Lodges.* London: Printed by William Hunter, for John Senex, and John Hooke, 1723.

—————————. *The New Book of Constitutions of the Antient and Honourable Fraternity of Free and Accepted Masons. Containing Their History, Charges, Regulations, &c. Collected and Digested by Order of The Grand Lodge from Their Old Records, Faithful Traditions and Lodge-Books, for the Use of the Lodges.* London: Printed for Brothers Cæsar Ward and Richard Chandler, Booksellers, at the Ship Without Temple-Bar; and Sold at Their Shops in Coney-Street, York, and at Scarborough-Spaw, 1738.

[Anon]. *A Defence of Free-Masonry, As Practiced in the Regular Lodges, Both Foreign and Domestic, Under the Constitution of the English Grand-Master.* London: Flexney and Hood, 1765.

Aquinas, St. Thomas of. *Summa Theologica*. Translated by Fathers of the English Dominican Province. London: Benziger Bros., 1947.

Baker, David Erskine. *An Oration in Honour of Free-Masonry. Delivered before the Honourable and Worshipful the Grand Lodge of Scotland. 30th November, 1763. Being St. Andrew's Day*. Edinburgh, 1763.

Beeson, Eric. "Andragogy," in *The SAGE Encyclopedia of Educational Research, Measurement, and Evaluation* (Thousand Oaks, Calif.: SAGE Publications, Inc, 2018), https://doi.org/10.4135/9781506326139.n43.

Black, Walter J., ed. *Complete Works of William Shakespeare*. New York: Walter J. Black, 1937.

Bullamore, George W. "The Beehive and Freemasonry." *Ars Quatuor Coronatorum* 36 (1923): 219–33.

Burton, Howard. *Mindsets: Growing Your Brain*. Toronto, Canada: Open Agenda Publishing, 2020.

Camlin, David A., Helena Daffern, and Katherine Zeserson. "Group Singing as a Resource for the Development of a Healthy Public: A Study of Adult Group Singing." *Humanities and Social Sciences Communications* 7, no. 1 (August 5, 2020): 1–15.

Campbell, Katherine. "Masonic Song in Scotland: Folk Tunes and Community." *Oral Tradition* 27, no. 1 (2012): 85–107.

Clarke, Arthur C. "Clarke's Third Law on UFO's." *Science* 159, no. 3812 (January 19, 1968): 255–255.

Claudy, Carl H. *The Master's Book*. Washington, D.C.: The Temple Publishers, 1935.

Cole, Benjamin. *The Antient Constitutions of the Free and Accepted Masons*. The second edition. London: printed for B. Creake, at the Red Bible in Ave-Mary-Lane, Ludgate-Street, near St. Paul's; and B. Cole Engraver, the Corner of King's Head-Court, near Fetter-Lane, Holbourn, 1731.

Coleman, Janet. *Ancient and Medieval Memories: Studies in the Reconstruction of the Past*. New York: Cambridge University Press, 1992.

Cox, Daniel A. "The State of American Friendship: Change, Challenges, and Loss." The Survey Center on American Life (blog), 2021.

https://www.americansurveycenter.org/research/the-state-of-american-friendship-change-challenges-and-loss/.

Cross, Jeremy Ladd. *The True Masonic Chart, or Hieroglyphic Monitor; Containing All the Emblems Explained in the Degrees.* New Haven, Conn.: T. Woodward, 1826.

D'Assigny, Fifield. *An Impartial Answer to the Enemies of Free-Masonry, wherein Their unjust Suspicions, and idle Reproaches of that Honourable Craft, are briefly Rehearsed, and clearly Confuted.* Dublin: Printed by Edward Waters in Dames' street and are to be sold at his Shop, and at Mr. Richard Pinder's at the White Hart in Pembroke Court, n.d. [1741].

Davies, Malcolm. *The Masonic Muse: Songs, Music and Musicians Associated with Dutch Freemasonry, 1730–1806.* Koninklijke Vereniging voor Nederlandse Muziekgeschiedenis, 2005.

Davis, Robert G. *The Mason's Words: The History and Evolution of the American Masonic Ritual* (Guthrie, Okla.: Building Stone Publishing, 2013.

Dermott, Laurence. *Ahiman Rezon: Or, A Help to a Brother; Shewing the Excellency of Secrecy, and the First Cause, or Motive, of the Institution of Free-Masonry [&c. Followed by] A Choice Collection of Masons Songs.* London: James Bedford, 1756.

Duncan, Malcom C. *Duncan's Masonic Ritual and Monitor.* New York: Dick & Fitzgerald, 1866.

Dunckerley, Thomas. *The Light and Truth of Masonry Explained, Being the Substance of a Charge Delivered at Plymouth, in April, 1757, by Thomas Dunckerley, Esq., P.G.M.* London: Davey & Law, 1757.

Dweck, Carol S. *Mindset: The New Psychology of Success.* New York: Ballantine Books, 2007.

Dyer, Colin F. W. *Symbolism in Craft Freemasonry.* Shepperton, UK: Lewis Masonic, 1976.

—————. *William Preston and His Work.* Shepperton, UK: Lewis Masonic, 1987.

Eyer, Shawn. "The Beehive and the Stock of Knowledge." *Philalethes:*

The Journal of Masonic Research & Letters 63, no. 1 (2010): 35–37, 42.

——————. "The Essential Secrets of Masonry: Insight from an American Masonic Oration of 1734." In *Exploring Early Grand Lodge Freemasonry: Studies in Honor of the Tricentennial of the Establishment of the Grand Lodge of England*, edited by Christopher B. Murphy and Shawn Eyer, 152–215. Washington, D.C.: Plumbstone Academic, 2017.

——————. "This Divine Science: Architecture and Speculative Freemasonry," The George Washington Masonic National Memorial (blog), 2015, https://gwmemorial.org/blogs/news/this-divine-science.

Gabor, Dennis. *Inventing the Future*. First Edition. London: Secker & Warburg, 1963.

Harris, Thaddeus Mason. *Constitutions of the Ancient and Honourable Fraternity of Free and Accepted Masons*. Worcester, Massachusetts: Isaiah Thomas, 1792.

Hobsbawm, Eric, and Terence Ranger, eds. *The Invention of Tradition*. Cambridge Cambridgeshire: Cambridge University Press, 1992.

Hunt, Charles C. *Masonic Concordance of the Holy Bible*. Bloomington, Illinois: Masonic Book Club, 1984.

Hutchens, Rex R., Ronald A. Seale, and Arturo de Hoyos. *A Bridge To Light: A Study In Masonic Ritual & Philosophy*. 4th edition. The Supreme Council of the Scottish Rite, 2021.

Jamison, Stephanie W., and Joel P. Brereton, eds. *The Rigveda: The Earliest Religious Poetry of India*. Oxford: Oxford University Press, 2014.

Kirk, Robert. *The Secret Commonwealth of Elves, Fauns, and Fairies*. Aberfoyle, England, 1691.

Knights of the North, The. "Laudable Pursuit II: Examining the Progress and Future of Regular Freemasonry in North America." 2019. https://theknightsofthenorth.org/wp-content/uploads/2019/06/Laudable-Pursuit-2.pdf.

Knowles, Malcolm S., Elwood F. Holton III, and Richard A. Swanson. *The Adult Learner: The Definitive Classic in Adult Education*

and Human Resource Development. Burlington, Ma.: Butterworth-Heinemann, 2005.

Leprohon, Ronald J. *The Great Name: Ancient Egyptian Royal Titulary*.
Atlanta, Ga.: Society of Biblical Literature, 2013.

Leslie, Charles. "A Vindication of Masonry, and its Excellency Demonstrated in a Discourse at the Consecration of the Lodge Vernon
Kilwinning, on May 15, 1741, by Charles Leslie, M.A. Master-Mason
and Member of that Lodge." In *The Free Masons Pocket-companion*, 153–64. Edinburgh: Printed by Auld, and Smellie, and sold at
their Printing House, Morocco's Close, Lawn-Market, M,DCC,LXV
[1765]).

Mackey, Albert. *The Symbolism of Freemasonry: Illustrating and Explaining its Science and Philosophy, its Legends, Myths, and Symbols*.
New York: Clark and Maynard, 1869.

MacNulty, W. Kirk. *Contemplating Craft Freemasonry: Working the
Way of the Craftsman*. Washington, D.C.: Plumbstone, 2017.

—————————. *Freemasonry: A Journey through Ritual and Symbol*.
London: Thames & Hudson, 1991.

—————————. *Freemasonry: Symbols, Secrets, Significance*. London: Thames & Hudson, 2006.

—————————. *The Way of the Craftsman: Deluxe Edition*. Washington, D.C.: Plumbstone, 2017.

Morgan, William. *Illustrations of Masonry, by One of the Fraternity,
Who Has Devoted Thirty Years to the Subject: With an Appendix,
Containing a Key to the Higher Degrees of Freemasonry; by a Mem-
ber of the Craft*. Cincinnati: Matthew Gardiner, 1826.

Masonic Service Association of North America. "U.S. Membership
Statistics — Masonic Service Association of North America," 2023.
https://msana.com/services/u-s-membership-statistics/.

Murphy, Christopher B. "Assessing Authentic Lodge Culture: Moving
Beyond the Tavern Myth." In *Exploring Early Grand Lodge Freemasonry: Studies in Honor of the Tricentennial of the Establishment of
the Grand Lodge of England*, edited by Christopher B. Murphy and

Shawn Eyer, 390–455. Washington, D.C.: Plumbstone Academic, 2017.

———. "The Mason's Faculty and the Language of Adam: An Untrod Path of Inquiry." *The Plumbline* 25, no. 4 (2018): 1, 3–7.

———. "The Tavern Myth: Reassessing the Culture of Early Grand Lodge Era Freemasonry," *Philalethes: The Journal of Masonic Research and Letters* 68, no. 2 (2015): 50–61.

Norman, Nick. "Why So Many Men Feel Lonely Today." *Psychology Today*, 2023.

Porphyry. *On the Cave of the Nymphs in the Thirteenth Book of the Odyssey*. Translated by Thomas Taylor. London: J. M. Watkins, 1917.

Preston, William. *Illustrations Of Masonry*. 2nd ed. London: Printed for J. Wilkie, No. 71. St. Paul's Church Yard, 1775.

———. *Illustrations Of Masonry*. 12th ed. London: Printed for G. Wilkie, No 57, Paternoster-Row, 1812.

———. *Illustrations of Masonry: A Grand Gala in Honour of Free Masonry, Held at the Crown and Anchor Tavern, in the Strand*. London: Brother J. Williams, opposite St. Dunstan's Church, Fleet Street., 1772.

Ransome, Hilda M. *The Sacred Bee in Ancient Times and Folklore*. London: George Allen & Unwin, 1937.

Robibo, Aviva. *The Guru Tradition: India's Spiritual Heritage*. New York: Lexington Books, 2024.

Allegra Rosenberg, "What If the Solution to Men's Loneliness Is . . . Freemasonry?" *Slate*, September 28, 2024, https://slate.com/life/2024/09/freemasons-lodges-conspiracies-membership-requirements.html.

Ruli, B. Christopher. *The White House and the Freemasons*. Richmond, Va.: Macoy, 2023.

Schuchard, Marsha Keith. "Swift, Ramsay, and 'the Cabala, as Masonry Was Call'd in Those Days.'" *English Language Notes* 56, no. 1 (2018): 97–118.

Sinclair, A. T. "The Secret Language of Masons and Tinkers." *The Jour-

nal of American Folklore 22, no. 86 (1909): 353–64.

Smith, Dwight. "Whither Are We Travelling." *Ars Quatuor Corona-torum, Being the Transactions of the Quatuor Coronati Lodge No. 2076* 76 (1963).

Smith, William. *The Book M: Or, Masonry Triumphant.* Newcastle upon Tyne: Printed by Leonard Umfreville and Company, 1736.

Speth, G.W. "A Masonic Curriculum." *Ars Quatuor Coronatorum, Being the Transactions of the Quatuor Coronati Lodge No. 2076* 3 (1890): 116–20.

St. Pierre, Nathan A. "'Genius of Masonry': The Preservation of Masonic Tradition in the Songs of the Freemasons." In *Exploring Early Grand Lodge Freemasonry: Studies in Honor of the Tricentennial of the Establishment of the Grand Lodge of England*, edited by Christopher B. Murphy and Shawn Eyer, 280–312. Washington, D.C.: Plumbstone Academic, 2017.

Tapley, Rev. *A Charge Delivered to the Brethren of the Most Ancient and Honourable Society of Free and Accepted Masons, Assembled at the King's-Head, in West-Street, Gravesend, on the 29th of June, at Their First Meeting after Their Constitution.* London, 1751.

Traynor, Kirsten. "The Tears of Re: Beekeeping in Ancient Egypt." *American Entomologist* 62, no. 3 (2016): 194–96.

Watts, Isaac. *Divine Songs Attempted in Easy Language for the Use of Children.* 2nd ed. London: printed for M. Lawrence at the Angel in the Poultry, 1716.

Webb, Thomas Smith. *The Freemason's Monitor; or, Illustrations of Masonry: In Two Parts.* Albany: Printed for Spencer and Webb, Market-Street, 1797.

—————. *The Freemason's Monitor; or, Illustrations of Masonry: In Two Parts.* New York: Printed by Southwick and Crooker No. 354, Water-Street, 1802.

Weiss, Avrum. "The High Cost of Men's Loneliness." *Psychology Today*, November 21, 2021. https://www.psychologytoday.com/us/blog/from-fear-to-intimacy/202111/the-high-cost-of-mens-loneliness

166

Wilmshurst, Walter Leslie. *The Masonic Initiation.* San Francisco: Plumbstone, 2007.

————————. *The Meaning of Masonry.* San Francisco: Plumbstone, 2007.

————————. *The Way to the East.* London: Watkins, 1938.

Wilson, William Ritchie. "The Truth of Haikai." *Monumenta Nipponica* 26, no. 1/2 (1971): 49–53.

Yates, Frances A. *The Art of Memory.* Chicago: University of Chicago Press, 1966.

Zaehner, R. C. *Hindu Scriptures.* New York: Everyman's Library, 1966.

About the Author

Nathan St. Pierre is a Past Master of The Lodge of the Nine Muses № 1776 in Washington, D.C., and now happily hives with Melbourne Lodge № 143 in Melbourne, Florida. He is the co-author, with Shawn Eyer, of *Sing the Art Divine: A Traditional Masonic Songster*.

www.ingramcontent.com/pod-product-compliance
Lightning Source LLC
Chambersburg PA
CBHW030013290326
41934CB00005B/326